GW01043918

FOR THE LOVE OF
LONDON

FOR THE LOVE OF LONDON

Summersdale Publishers Ltd
46 West Street
Chichester
West Sussex
PO19 1RP
UK

www.summersdale.com

Printed and bound in the Czech Republic

ISBN: 978-1-78685-001-0

Substantial discounts on bulk quantities of Summersdale books are available to corporations, professional associations and other organisations. For details contact general enquiries: telephone: +44 (0) 1243 771107, fax: +44 (0) 1243 786300 or email: enquiries@summersdale.com.

FOR THE LOVE OF
LONDON

A COMPANION

JULIAN BEECROFT

summersdale

This book is for Ulla, my London girl

CONTENTS

INTRODUCTION: THE GLOBAL CITY

London must have a fair claim to being the greatest city on Earth. In summer 2016, it displaced New York City as the place where the global rich and famous most wanted to live – or at least to place their money – and where large numbers of the world's brightest and most ambitious people longed to settle and make their names.

According to one index, it is one of two alpha ++ global cities – a ranking it earns from the pivotal role it plays in so many aspects of the world economy, from cultural exchange to business activity, from its ability to attract the best brains to the capacity of its businesses and institutions to innovate across so many fields.

But these statistics don't get near to explaining why London is also the most visited city in the Western world and, at the time of writing, the second most visited on the planet after Bangkok. Being so hard to pin down is perhaps the very quality that draws people to London in the first place, as the city seems so much greater than our ability to comprehend it, not only in size but in scope.

There are certain natural advantages which, even in prehistoric times, made the current site of London the most obvious place for a principal settlement on the island of Britain (as we now know it), and later the most natural place in the country for a capital: its location on the banks of a broad and navigable river that flowed swiftly to the sea and back as, twice a day, the tide went out and came in again. In 2010, a survey of the foreshore at Vauxhall found evidence of a bridge some 6,000 years old, in the form of six timber piles sticking out of the mud, close to the site of a later wooden structure, a mere 3,500 years old, that now partly resides in the Museum of London. It was and has remained ever since a perfect place for trade, even if in that regard the river has lost its pre-eminent role in the past half-century. Britain remains what it has always been – a great trading nation – and it has always taken its lead from London.

ROMAN LONDON

By the time of the Roman conquest of Britain in AD 43, areas close to the river had been inhabited for thousands of years. The Romans, always quick to see a strategic advantage, founded the capital of the new province of Britannia on the same site and gave it the name Londinium. The city grew quickly to a place of 20,000 souls and became the hub of a series of characteristically straight Roman roads reaching out to all parts of the province.

Those parts of the old London Wall that can still be seen, such as the original section next to the Museum of London, date back to the Romans, as does the amphitheatre discovered and now – partly and rather brilliantly – displayed in the basement of the **Guildhall Art Gallery** in the City of London. This is not unusual: as the modern City continues to expand, mostly upwards, new foundations are sunk into parts of the subsoil that have lain undisturbed for millennia so new discoveries are continually being made. However, despite many Britons acknowledging what the Romans had done for them, bringing the cultural and human variety of the first global empire to this cold northern outpost, not everyone was happy.

DISASTERS: THE ORIGINAL GREAT FIRE OF LONDON

Queen Boudicca, a heroine of British history, was no lover of the global power of Rome and the international community of immigrant workers and elite non-doms that populated Roman London. She had good reason to despise an occupying power which had annexed her kingdom and whose soldiers had raped her own daughters, so in AD 61 she led a raid on Londinium. She torched and sacked this cosmopolitan city, killing 30,000 Londoners and burning it to the ground. She and her people, the Iceni, paid dearly for the uprising, but she earned a place in folklore as the original champion of British liberty against the oppressive might of European imperial power – whether real or imagined! But just as this instinct is ingrained in the national character, so an indelible trait since that first cosmopolis is the irrepressible energy of London, its bouncebackability, the self-interested wisdom of its openness to the world. So it was that just a few years after what we might call the first Great Fire, Londinium had re-established itself as the dominant city in Roman Britain, famous according to the Roman writer Tacitus for 'its concourse of merchants and for the abundance of its provisions'.

SAXON LONDON

The Romans built the first London Bridge on the site of the current bridge, as we know from the remains of a wooden pier, dating back to *c.* AD 85, discovered at Pudding Lane in the heart of the City. After a further great fire in AD 122, which wiped out most of the early Roman city, a newly rebuilt Londinium thrived, reaching a peak population of some 60,000 people – a number that would not be exceeded until the Middle Ages. But after the Romans left in AD 410, the city declined to such an extent that by the end of the fifth century fewer than 1,000 people were left in the area. For the next few hundred years, the old city was abandoned and a settlement named Lundenwic (meaning 'London marketplace') grew up on the site of today's Covent Garden – controlled by first the East Saxons and then the Mercians – whose population by AD 750 had grown to some 8,000 people.

Attacks by Vikings in the mid-ninth century led to the new town's occupation by the Danes, but the place simply had too much going for it for the Saxons, once an immigrant people themselves, to accept this theft of their greatest urban asset. In 880 or thereabouts, after just a few decades in the hands of the invaders, King Alfred recaptured the site with his Saxon army and gave it yet another change of name: to Lundenburh or Lundenburg. Over the following century or so it would gradually become the nation's permanent seat of government, as well as its principal city of trade.

ALONG THE RIVER: TEDDINGTON LOCK TO RICHMOND

One of the best ways to properly appreciate the history and character of London is by travelling the length of the river that runs through it from Teddington to the Thames Estuary. Once an artery of energetic trade and now mostly a peaceful conduit of leisure, the tidal Thames begins 68 miles from the sea at **Teddington Lock**, on the outer edge of southwest London. The first fixed crossing over the tidal river beyond the lock, **Richmond Bridge** dates from the late eighteenth century and is the oldest surviving of London's many bridges. By the time we reach it we have already passed through Strawberry Hill. This is the site of **Strawberry Hill House**: Horace Walpole's eighteenth-century Gothic revival fantasy, whose style would do so much to shape the aesthetic of Victorian London.

As we come through Twickenham, we pass by **Eel Pie Island**, which in the 1960s was the site of the Eel Pie Island Hotel, one of the more vibrant music venues in the capital, with The Who and The Rolling Stones among the acts to have played there. Further downriver, on the way to the bridge, two fine houses can be seen on opposite banks: first **Ham House** on the Richmond (or Surrey) side, a Jacobean mansion regarded as one of the finest surviving houses of the period. Then we find **Marble Hill House**, an elegant villa built a century later in the Palladian style, on the Twickenham (or Middlesex) side. A ferry service, **Hammerton's**

Ferry, takes pedestrians and cyclists across the narrow stretch of river in this southwestern part of London. The other such ferry on the London Thames is the **Woolwich Ferry** which runs across the very wide river beyond the Thames Barrier at the city's eastern limit.

Leaving Richmond Bridge behind us, we soon pass the site of Richmond Palace, the favourite residence of Queen Elizabeth I and one of the first buildings anywhere to be fitted with a flushing toilet, designed by Elizabeth's godson, Sir John Harrington. Today only a few minor elements of the original complex of buildings remain standing; it was demolished and its building materials sold off in the 1650s during the short-lived English Commonwealth presided over by Oliver Cromwell.

WORSHIPPING LONDON

A visitor walking around London in the centuries before and even after the Great Fire of 1666 might have been impressed above all by the number of churches in this city famous for trade and commerce. But, as we know from the remains of the Temple of Mithras at Walbrook discovered in 1954, religious buildings have always been an integral part of the fabric of London. And while the great age of church building might have passed, some of London's most breathtaking modern structures are religious buildings dedicated to other faiths, whose communities form a strong part of the social fabric of modern London. So while it's hard to imagine the capital without its many churches, it's even harder to think of modern London without its many faiths.

ST PAUL'S CATHEDRAL

At the top of Ludgate Hill, the highest point in the City of London, stands St Paul's Cathedral, perhaps the building that for centuries was seen as the symbol of the capital, both by Londoners and people around the world. In fact, the current cathedral is the fourth to have stood on this site, the first three having been destroyed by the great fires of 961, 1087 and, most famously, 1666. The present building only escaped the same fate, by what some would describe as a miracle, in the great fire of 29 December 1940, when the Luftwaffe bombed the historic areas of the City of London around St Paul's, destroying many churches and historic buildings.

Designed by Sir Christopher Wren, St Paul's is the outstanding masterpiece of English Baroque architecture. It is notable for its harmonious marriage of the general plan common to most English medieval cathedrals – with a transept and a long nave – and the elegant European sophistication of the buildings by which Wren was inspired: in particular, François Mansart's Church of the Val-de-Grâce in Paris and Michelangelo's Basilica of St Peter's in Rome.

Wren had already taken on the rebuilding, to his own new designs, of more than 50 of the City's parish churches after the Great Fire when this most prestigious of commissions was also entrusted to him. Such an important building brought with it all kinds of expectations from members of the clergy as to what an Anglican cathedral should look like. Several of Wren's earlier designs were rejected, including the one for which the 'Great Model' was made in 1674 to demonstrate his ideas; visitors can still view this marvellous 1:25 scale alternative at the cathedral today. And even the finished building drew objections, as the ingenious central double-skinned dome, when first proposed, was considered by some a particularly 'popish' invention. The circular promenade that runs around the interior of the base of the dome is known as the Whispering Gallery, on account of peculiar acoustics which make it possible to hear someone speaking very quietly on the opposite side.

Many of Britain's most famous men (though very few women) are buried or commemorated at St Paul's, including Wren himself, as well as some of London's most famous sons, such as the painter J. M. W. Turner, the poet and painter William Blake, and the poet John Donne, who for the latter part of his life was Dean of Old St Paul's. In the crypt the nation's two most renowned military men, the Duke of Wellington and Lord Nelson, lie in impressive sarcophagi reflecting their exalted status in British history.

The cathedral is also a working church, and in living memory it has played host to some of the nation's most solemn public events, such as the funerals of Sir Winston Churchill and the former prime minister, Margaret Thatcher, not to mention the wedding in 1981 of Prince Charles and Lady Diana Spencer.

WREN CHURCHES

Aside from St Paul's, of the 54 churches that Wren designed as part of the rebuilding of London after the Great Fire, 26 still stand which either survived the Blitz and earlier Victorian destruction or else were reconstructed after World War Two. The variety of these structures, conceived and built at an astonishing rate during the 1670s and 1680s, is testament to the fecundity of Wren's genius. Among the most interesting are **St Bride's** in Fleet Street, known as the Journalists' Church, which with its distinctive tall spire resembles a many-tiered pagoda, making it the second-highest of Wren's churches after St Paul's. Then there are **St Stephen's, Walbrook**, with its beautiful domed interior, and **St Mary-le-Bow**, whose great bell is remembered in 'Oranges and Lemons', the famous nursery rhyme about the City's churches. Traditionally, anyone born within earshot of 'Bow Bells' is entitled to call themselves a Cockney, but given the level of noise and the absence of housing in the modern hub of global finance that is the City of London today, that must make Cockneys a tribe on the brink of going extinct.

WESTMINSTER ABBEY

Westminster Abbey is the finest Gothic building in London and, in constitutional terms, the most important religious building in England – a status reflected in its description as a 'Royal Peculiar', making the Dean of the Abbey answerable directly to the Queen and not to any bishop or even to the Archbishop of Canterbury himself. Constructed over a period of almost three centuries, the abbey has the highest nave of any English church, while the fan-vaulted ceiling of the Lady Chapel – begun in the reign of Henry VII – is one of the marvels of English architecture. But as with St

Paul's, its history dates back to Saxon times, when a Benedictine abbey was built on the site of what was then an island in the Thames, known as Thorney Island. Edward the Confessor, the most devout of English kings and a bona fide Catholic saint, had his palace adjacent to the abbey on the current site of the Houses of Parliament. In 1042, inspired by a dream, he instructed that the existing abbey be replaced with an abbey church, which was referred to as the 'West Minster', or west monastery, to distinguish it from the cathedral of St Paul's, further downriver to the east.

Edward the Confessor died in January 1066, and Harold Godwinson is likely to have been crowned there a week or so later, as was his successor, William of Normandy – the man who defeated Harold at the Battle of Hastings – before the same year was out. Indeed, one of its greatest treasures testifies to its special role in the national story. The Coronation Chair made for Edward I, conqueror of Wales, is a huge oaken throne designed to incorporate the famous Stone of Scone beneath its seat. This sacred rock – also known as the Stone of Destiny – has been venerated by Scots for a thousand years but was stolen by King Edward in 1296 specifically to take its appointed place beneath the seat of the Coronation Chair. Since then, every English or British monarch – aside from Edward V in the fifteenth century and Edward VIII in the twentieth century – including Elizabeth II, the present Queen, has been crowned in that chair. However, in 1996 the UK's then-Prime Minister, John Major, instructed that the stone be returned to Scotland on the understanding it would be loaned back whenever it was needed in the future.

The current building, whose proper name is the Collegiate Church of St Peter, Westminster, was begun in the thirteenth century on the orders of Henry III. Over almost five centuries from the death of that same monarch, Henry III, in 1272 to that of George II in 1760, the abbey was the burial place of the majority of English kings and queens; the Protestant Elizabeth I and Mary I – her predecessor, rival and Catholic half-sister – are both buried in one of the numerous side chapels: and in the same tomb to boot, an indignity that no male monarch has had to endure! But the area most beloved by visitors is probably Poets' Corner, which reads like the Contents page of an anthology of the greatest British writers, either buried or commemorated in this spot: from Chaucer and Shakespeare to Jane Austen and all three Brontë sisters, and most recently, the great nature poet Ted Hughes.

HAWKSMOOR CHURCHES

In fact, Westminster Abbey was only finally finished in 1745, with the addition of the two distinctive west towers. The architect who designed them, Nicholas Hawksmoor, had died almost a decade earlier, but his legacy can still be seen all over the capital: in the work he did as assistant to Wren on St Paul's, the new apartments for King William III at Hampton Court Palace, the ensemble of buildings for the Greenwich Hospital and the six highly original churches for whose design he was wholly responsible, whose eclecticism and inventiveness were far ahead of their time. These are mostly in the City and the East End: **Christ Church Spitalfields,** which has a Gothic steeple but a portico that uses classical elements, **St George in the East** at Wapping, with its castellated spire and smaller corner towers which, according to one observer, resemble pepper pots, and **St Mary Woolnoth,** close to the Bank of England, whose eccentric flat façade makes for an imposing wall of stone but whose interior is flooded with light.

TEMPLE CHURCH

Though the churches of Wren and Hawksmoor have come to define the church architecture of the parishes of old London, they are not the full story, as not every medieval church was destroyed in the Great Fire of 1666. Among the survivors, one of the oldest is Temple Church, which sits in a quiet courtyard between Fleet Street and the River Thames, in the heart of London's legal district. It has found new fame in recent years as an element in the plot of Dan Brown's worldwide bestseller *The Da Vinci Code,* but its own storied history is fascinating even without the fictitious boost.

Built by the mysterious Knights Templar – a monastic order of soldiers – upon their return from the second Crusade, the oldest part of the current building, the Round Church which now acts as a nave, was in use by 1162. Its shape was designed to mimic and recreate the sanctity of the Church of the Holy Sepulchre in Jerusalem, the city which for Christians is the centre of the world and whose defence was the order's central purpose.

During the period of the Crusades, the Templars enjoyed enormous influence and held all the lands around the church between Fleet Street and the river, the site of the numerous legal chambers of today's Inner and Middle Temples. These monks-cum-fighting men acted as bankers and diplomatic brokers to successive kings, but were on the wrong side of history when in 1215 they supported King John in his failed attempt to resist the demands of the rebel barons, which led that summer to Magna Carta.

The church's rectangular chancel was added in 1240, but at the start of the fourteenth century the order was abolished by Pope Clement V. Two centuries on, King James I restored the Templars to some position of influence in England, allowing them to regain their former lands in London on condition that the two Inns of Court which occupied the land undertake to maintain the church itself in perpetuity 'for the celebration of divine service'.

ST PAUL'S, COVENT GARDEN

In the heart of Covent Garden, at the centre of London's theatre district, sits St Paul's Church, known to Londoners as the Actors' Church. Finished in 1633, and thus predating Wren's achievements by several decades, it was designed by Inigo Jones – the man responsible for introducing the ideas of Italian Renaissance architect Andrea Palladio to Britain – though the exterior of the temple-like building of St Paul's follows the ideas of the early Roman architect Vitruvius (first century BC).

In fact, Jones was responsible for designing the whole of London's first public square, Covent Garden Piazza, which became a huge influence on the future layout of London, of which St Paul's is the only surviving building along the western side. These days the classical portico facing onto the square, blocked up since it was built, often serves as a backdrop to the street performers who ply their trade in the bustling heart of Covent Garden, while the peaceful rose garden leading up to the entrance, at the back of the church, has long been a favourite place for people working in the area to take their lunch.

ST MARTIN-IN-THE-FIELDS

St Martin-in-the-Fields, in the northeastern corner of Trafalgar Square, has been the site of a church possibly since Roman times. Fields did indeed surround it right up until the Tudor period, before the area between the respective cities of London and Westminster was developed. The church is a Neoclassical design by James Gibbs, completed in 1726. In 2008, a new East Window was unveiled to replace one damaged in the bombing of World War Two; featuring a warped, ovum-shaped central lacuna by Iranian artist Shirazeh Houshiary, it transcends any religious affiliation and is one of the outstanding permanent works of modern art in London.

Beneath the church is the spacious crypt, which hosts a café long-favoured by Londoners as somewhere to get good, cheap, hearty food. And the presence of so many of central London's homeless people in the nearby streets points to Connection at St Martin's, the capital's largest homeless charity, which offers a range of services including a day and a night shelter in a nearby building.

Like Temple Church and many other religious buildings in London, St Martin's also hosts a thriving programme of classical music concerts. The Academy of St Martin in the Fields, one of the world's leading chamber orchestras, gave its maiden performance in the church in 1959 under the direction of its founder, the conductor Sir Neville Marriner.

ALL SAINTS MARGARET STREET

All Saints Margaret Street is one of London's architectural wonders, a brick-built High Anglican church constructed on a tiny plot just 100 square feet on a side street just off the northern end of Regent Street. It was commissioned in the 1840s by the Ecclesiological Society, who wanted: a 'model Church on a large and splendid scale', whose architect should be 'a single, pious and laborious artist alone, pondering deeply over his duty to do his best for the service of God's Holy Religion'. That 'artist' was William Butterfield and All Saints is his masterpiece.

Designed in 1850 in the Gothic Revival style and completed in 1859, it is all the more astonishing in that the desired 'model church on a splendid scale' would have to contend with surrounding buildings in close proximity and thus a very confined site with a restricted amount of natural light. As a result, there are fewer windows than normal for a church of this size, and these are mostly high up. What makes All Saints truly remarkable is the decoration of seemingly every available surface – not just the stained-glass windows but the walls, floor and ceilings – with a bewildering array of decorative strategies: narrative biblical scenes on the walls of the nave using coloured ceramic tiles, paintings on gilded boards in the chancel and the intricate tiled patterns of the floors. The patterning begins on the outside of the church in the use of red and black bricks – previously a material chosen for less important buildings – in a decorative scheme that was built into the structure and would exert a big influence on later Victorian architecture.

BEVIS MARKS SYNAGOGUE

Bevis Marks is London's oldest and most beautiful synagogue. It is also the only synagogue in Europe to have been in continuous use for more than 300 years. Founded in 1701 by the Sephardi community of Spanish and Portuguese Jews, the building occupies a site in the heart of the City, just around the corner from 30 St Mary Axe, otherwise known as the Gherkin. Miraculously, it managed to get through the Blitz unscathed, but in 1992 it was badly damaged by an IRA bomb that targeted the Baltic Exchange, which used to stand on the site now occupied by the Gherkin. It has since been restored and is still used by British Jews for major ceremonies, also serving a modern congregation from all over the world who work in the City, thus earning it the sobriquet 'The Synagogue in the Square Mile'.

BROMPTON ORATORY

Brompton Oratory, officially the Church of the Immaculate Heart of Mary, is the second-largest Catholic church after Westminster Cathedral and probably the most impressive in London. Situated on the Brompton Road, right next to the Victoria and Albert Museum, the Oratory's wonderful atmosphere is in part due to the many roof lanterns that flood its vast spaces from above with broad shafts of natural light. Drawing on the Baroque religious architecture of Rome, the interior makes lavish use of marble. The Oratory is also a great centre of Catholic music, with three internationally acclaimed choirs who specialise in the performance of liturgical music.

WESTMINSTER CATHEDRAL

The neo-Byzantine Westminster Cathedral is the largest Catholic church, and the faith's mother church, in England and Wales. Completed in 1903, it is particularly striking for the striped red-and-white brick exterior, while the interior is decorated in places with mosaics in the Byzantine style. However, even today it remains a work in progress, as many of the cavernous internal spaces are still bare, undecorated brick. As with the Brompton Oratory, the

Cathedral choir is world-renowned not only for its performances of the traditional repertoire of choral polyphony, but also for the new works it has commissioned and performed from the likes of Sir James MacMillan and Sir Peter Maxwell Davies.

NEASDEN TEMPLE

The BAPS Shri Swaminarayan Mandir, popularly known as the Neasden Temple, could well be the most beautiful and certainly the most astonishing building in London. Visitors approaching it along a quiet suburban street in northwest London could be forgiven for thinking they had passed through some secret portal into another continent. Drawing on the traditional religious architecture of the Hindu faith in India, the temple's six domes and nine pinnacles crown a building that is 195 feet long and 70 feet high.

Just as astonishing were the circumstances of its creation. The process of designing and building the temple was astoundingly rapid. During a period of mere months, a design was conceived and funds were raised, so that huge quantities of marble and limestone could be purchased from quarries in Italy and Bulgaria respectively. European stone was favoured over Indian, so as to cope with the colder climate, but the quarried stone – some 5,000 tonnes of it – was then shipped to India where the intricate carving that so staggers the eye of all those who see it was executed by roughly 1,500 sculptors. The finished temple was brought back to Britain in 80 shipping containers holding

72,000 numbered pieces, which were then assembled in order with incredible speed by more than 1,000 volunteers. The entire process from conception to completion took a mere 27 months.

As a piece of architecture, the Neasden Temple cannot be compared with anything in Europe. Princess Diana and Prince Charles both separately testified to the spirit of devotion with which it was built and which it still reflects, while British businessman Sir Richard Branson has described it as 'one of the wonders of the world'. As a focus of the faith of the hundreds of thousands of Hindus who have made London their home over the last few decades, it also speaks volumes about the cultural breadth of modern London.

LONDON CENTRAL MOSQUE

Just around the corner from Lord's Cricket Ground is the shining golden dome of the Central London Mosque. One of over 400 mosques in London, the Regent's Park Mosque, as it is also known, was designed by Sir Frederick Gibberd and completed in 1978 as an annex to an existing building, the Islamic Cultural Centre, built in 1944, after the British wartime government of Sir Winston Churchill made a gift of the land on the park's western edge. At that time, London had the largest Muslim population of any European city, the result of immigration from an empire that comprised more Muslim subjects than Christian ones. Today, the centre professes to be the most active such Muslim institution in the Western world.

NORMAN
AND MEDIEVAL
LONDON

The conquest of England by William's Norman army saw the end of Saxon rule but wasn't all that bad for London. For a start, the city acquired its current name, though it took a few centuries for the spelling to settle into the form we use now. William, a smart king as well as a ruthless one, was quick to recognise the city's great strength as a centre of trade and commerce. Thus, in 1067, the year after the defeat of King Harold II, the Norman despot had the good sense to grant London a royal charter, which protected the rule of law the city had already established. In a further sign of royal favour, the city was later excluded from the Domesday Book, the nationwide inventory of assets whose compilation the king ordered in 1085.

A century later, French immigrants to Plantagenet London seeking to protect their commercial interests put forward the idea of a self-governing city, which led to the appointment in

1189 of Henry FitzAilwin as London's first mayor. However, while commercially London prospered, politically it could be volatile. In the same year, Henry II died and Richard I – the 'Lion Heart', as he was known – was crowned king. London's Jewish population had grown steadily after Jews had begun to settle in England following the Conquest of 1066. In an attempt to pledge their loyalty to the Crusader monarch, some of London's Jewish community made representations at the coronation, but were refused and from this rebuttal a rumour spread that the new king had in fact decreed a wholesale massacre. The same day, the Jews of London were set upon by a large and angry mob, slaughtered in their homes or, where they managed to bolt themselves in, burned alive. According to the later account of the eighteenth-century philosopher and historian David Hume, these atrocities involved 'so many of the most considerable citizens, that it was deemed more prudent to drop the prosecution'.

Of course, such outbreaks of anti-Semitism were not unique to London and became all too common in Europe during the medieval period. The capital still thrived, despite the barbarism, as it grew into a truly international city of trade with eventual links to the Hanseatic cities, the Mediterranean and even further afield, and its population increased by more than threefold between 1100 and 1348, from 25,000 to 80,000 people. Then disaster struck again.

DISASTERS: THE BLACK DEATH

London had experienced at least eight major fires in the century and a half between 1077 and 1229, causing significant destruction; Southwark on the south bank of the Thames was not yet part of London, but thousands died in the great fire of 1212 on that side of the river. However, by the mid-1340s a far more deadly scourge was advancing rapidly across Continental Europe, enabled by the ever-expanding trade networks of the Middle Ages, especially those going by sea. The growing fleets of larger ships brought diseases as well as commodities, and in August 1348, the deadliest of them all arrived in London: the Black Death – also called 'the great pestilence' or bubonic plague – transmitted by the rats that lived in the many thatched roofs of the medieval city. The epidemic killed an estimated 50 million people across Europe in the later 1340s and the early part of the next decade. By 1350, when the plague had finally subsided in London, the city's population of 80,000 had been reduced to half that number – and it was further depleted by several more plagues before the end of the following century.

ALONG THE RIVER: RICHMOND TO HAMMERSMITH BRIDGE

From Richmond the river passes under Twickenham Bridge and then, after Isleworth, slips past the extensive grounds of Kew Gardens, one of London's four UNESCO World Heritage Sites and still a place of significant research for botanical science. Rounding the Chiswick bend via one meander, we head in the other direction towards the next – the Barnes or Surrey bend – which is crossed by Hammersmith Bridge, one of the most elegant of all the crossings over the Thames.

Just before it, on the Hammersmith side, are two of London's best riverside pubs. **The Blue Anchor**, which opened in 1722, was a regular haunt of the composer Gustav Holst some 200 years later, while just before it is the **Dove**, an establishment of similar vintage that boasts the distinction of having the smallest bar of any pub in the United Kingdom. Up ahead, the current Hammersmith Bridge – the pale-green wrought-iron suspension bridge designed by the great Victorian engineer Joseph Bazalgette – replaced an earlier structure built in 1827, which by the 1870s was no longer able to bear the weight of traffic that thronged the streets of the imperial capital, even as far out as Hammersmith. Bazalgette's bridge has also suffered its fair share of problems over time, as by the 1980s the steady growth in the size of vehicles was causing structural problems. In 1997 this led to the closure of the bridge to cars and lorries; it reopened the following year with weight restrictions that remain in place today.

For some unknown reason, the bridge has been a favourite target of terrorist bombs over the years. In 2000, it was damaged by a device planted by the Real IRA, while four years earlier, the Provisional IRA had tried (and thankfully failed) to detonate the largest Semtex bomb ever seen in the UK. Fifty-seven years earlier, in 1939, it was again the IRA who had planted a bomb that was noticed by Maurice Childs, a local hairdresser who happened to be crossing the bridge in the early hours of the morning. Seeing a suitcase that was spewing smoke and spitting out sparks, he picked it up and hurled it into the river. As it hit the water, the bomb exploded, sending a 60-foot column of water into the air, moments before another bomb went off on the other side of the bridge, causing quite a bit of damage.

A LONDON CALENDAR

There is always some fair or festival, parade or sporting event going on in London, which is nothing less than you'd expect for a city of this size; the more activity and the more diversity, the more there is to celebrate or display. Some of these events, such as the **Frieze art fair** or the long-running **Ideal Home Show**, are as much annual opportunities for trade as they are spectacles for their own sake, while others, such as the Trooping the Colour ceremony or the Lord Mayor's Show, are pure pageantry.

Those last two have survived through centuries, whereas others, such as the great Bartholomew Fair, held at Smithfield in the City, or Southwark Fair – its counterpart south of the river – have passed into history. In the case of the famous frost fairs that took place in severe winters from the seventeenth to the early nineteenth centuries on the iced-over Thames itself, in the Pool of London below London Bridge, warming of the climate has rendered them physically impossible, especially after the medieval bridge was demolished and rebuilt in 1831, allowing water to flow more freely downriver through the new, more spaciously supported structure. The closest Londoners can now get to that spectacle of ice and fun are the temporary ice rinks that in recent years have set up shop every winter either side of Christmas at **Somerset House** on the Strand or in the courtyard of the Natural History Museum in South Kensington.

The sporting spectacles, on the other hand, are now better than they have ever been. They take place in state-of-the-art football stadia for club giants such as Arsenal, at the 60,000-seater **Emirates Stadium,** West Ham, at the 2012 Olympic Stadium – renamed the **London Stadium** – Tottenham at **White Hart Lane** or Chelsea at **Stamford Bridge.** And let's not forget the capital's many rugby stadia, especially the 82,000-seater **Twickenham Stadium,** where all England's home internationals are held. The following is a sample of the annual calendar of London's major events, many of them famous around the world.

THE LORD MAYOR'S SHOW

Although the first London mayor was appointed in 1189, it wasn't until 1215 that, under pressure from his barons, King John granted a royal charter to London, permitting them to elect their own mayor rather than accept an official appointed by the king. So on Michaelmas Day (29 September) or the closest weekday every year, the serving Lord Mayor convenes a gathering of liverymen from the City's 110 mostly ancient livery companies to elect the next Lord Mayor, who is then sworn in in November, the day before the Lord Mayor's Show.

The Lord Mayor's procession follows the same route it has taken for the past 800 years: from the City of London to Westminster, where traditionally the new Lord Mayor has pledged allegiance to the monarch of the day. The procession is headed by the two traditional guardians of the City, Gog and Magog, 14-foot giants made of wickerwork and pasteboard whose origins go back to medieval legends of ancient British kings. Behind them, the Mayor rides in the state coach, which is 350 years old and, when not in use, a prize exhibit at the Museum of London.

The most famous Lord Mayor of all was the late fourteenth-century mercer Richard (aka Dick) Whittington. Mercers imported luxury materials from Italy, the most advanced European culture of the time. Having arrived in London as a young lad, and been apprenticed to a mercer, Whittington soon rose to become an important merchant in his own right, in 1392 providing King Richard II with £3,000 worth of goods. Not a bad bit of business, especially as in 1397, by royal prerogative, the King suspended the City's customary practice of electing its own mayor and appointed Whittington to the post, renewing his tenure for the following year. He seems not to have done badly in the role, as the liverymen decided to elect him themselves twice more, in 1406 and 1419.

LONDON FASHION WEEK

London Fashion Week has been running for more than 30 years and is now one of the 'Big Four' fashion weeks alongside those of Milan, New York and Paris. It takes place twice a year, in February and September, with the aim of showcasing the spring/summer and autumn/winter collections, by mainly young British or British-based designers. As such, the clothes shown at LFW have always had the reputation of being edgier than those seen at long-established European centres of fashion. This reflects the street style of London itself, where most of the designers are based. Events are held at various locations around the city, but the main venue is Somerset House – specifically a marquee in the courtyard, where the most important catwalk shows are held. In September 2016, some 177 designers showed their latest collections during the week, hoping to catch the eye of stores and buyers keen to find the next big thing.

THE BOAT RACE

The Boat Race between crews of rowers representing the universities of Oxford and Cambridge dates back to 1829 and since 1856 has been held every year outside the two world wars. The main and oldest race is between two crews of 'heavyweight eights', effectively a men's race; there are also a reserve race and a women's race in the regatta, the latter fixture having been contested some 70 times. As of 2016, Cambridge had won the main race on 82 occasions to Oxford's 79 – a closeness that reflects the ultracompetitive nature of the contest.

The course, known as the Championship Course, has been the same every year since 1864: a 4 mile 374 yard stretch of the Thames rowing upstream between Putney and Mortlake in southwest London. It sounds a long way but the winning time these days is usually under 20 minutes, with the course record being a lung-busting 16 minutes and 19 seconds, set by the victorious Cambridge crew in 1998.

The races usually take place in late March or early April and are watched by around 250,000 people lining both banks of the river; since 1938 the race has been televised every year and nowadays draws an audience of some 15 million people. The only non-international boat race to be televised, it has also served up some classic moments, such as the closest-ever finish in the 2003 race, when Oxford won by just a foot, and the infamous 1978 race, when atrocious conditions that day caused the Cambridge boat to sink.

LONDON MARATHON

The London Marathon, which takes place in April every year, is the newest major event on London's sporting calendar. The first race, held in 1981, involved around 6,700 competitors; in 2010 nearly six times that number crossed the finishing line. The whole event involves a wheelchair race, a women's race and a men's race.

The marathon begins in southeast London at three separate points near Greenwich, and the course takes the runners past numerous London landmarks: past the *Cutty Sark*, down to Surrey Docks and over Tower Bridge; then east to Docklands and Canary Wharf, and back towards the City, passing the Tower of London. Next, runners head along the Victoria Embankment, passing Elizabeth Tower (Big Ben) and the Palace of Westminster, before reaching the final short stretch along Birdcage Walk to Buckingham Palace and heading back up the Mall to the finish line by St James's Palace.

FA CUP FINAL, WEMBLEY STADIUM

The FA Cup Final – the last match in the oldest football tournament in the world – takes place each year on a weekend in the middle of May. The first Football Association Challenge Cup tournament was held in 1871–72. Half a century later it moved to its spiritual home, Wembley Stadium, for the 1923 final between Bolton Wanderers and West Ham United. The game was attended by more than 240,000 people, twice the intended capacity, and has since become known as the White Horse Final for the white police horse that saved the day by pushing back the spectators thronging the pitch so that the fixture could go ahead. Thereafter, the FA Cup Final took place at Wembley every year – aside from the six years of World War Two – until the old stadium was demolished in 2000. For the next six years the Cup Final moved to the Millennium Stadium in Cardiff, Wales, while a new Wembley was built.

The new stadium, designed by Foster and Partners (and Populous), features an eye-catching steel lattice arch, now just as much of an icon as the Twin Towers that once adorned the old venue. The FA Cup Final and now the semi-finals are all based at the new Wembley, as are the home international fixtures of the England football team. The new stadium is also used in the same variety of ways as the old one, with other sporting events such as the rugby league Challenge Cup final and a series of NFL American football matches taking place there, as well as concerts given by major pop and rock stars with the pulling power to fill a 90,000-seat venue.

CHELSEA FLOWER SHOW

The Chelsea Flower Show, held every year in late May, is the most celebrated garden festival in the world. Being awarded a medal for their exhibit – especially a gold medal – is a prestigious accolade for any garden designer or plantsman, while garden lovers around the world consider attending the show as a kind of pilgrimage.

In fact, as the Royal Horticultural Society Great Spring Show, the event had been running in various venues around London for almost 80 years before, in 1912, it made its first appearance at the Royal Hospital, Chelsea. Aside from the temporary interruptions caused by two world wars, it has continued to be held there ever since, becoming so popular that since the late 1980s visitor numbers have had to be restricted to keep the crowding to a tolerable level. In response to the rising popularity of garden shows, the RHS has taken to staging other shows around the country, such as the Hampton Court Flower Show. The largest in the world, it is also the second most prestigious after Chelsea and takes place in early July in the grounds of the famous palace in southwest London.

TROOPING THE COLOUR

A big part of London's appeal to visitors is the persistence of traditions such as Trooping the Colour, which happens every year on a Saturday in June, close to the Queen's official birthday (her real birthday is 21 April). The ceremony dates back to the reign of Charles II in the late seventeenth century, a relic of a time when each regiment would carry its colours into battle to act as a rallying point amidst the fog of war.

The itinerary each year is reassuringly familiar. The Queen sets off from Buckingham Palace in mid-morning and proceeds down the Mall to Horse Guards Parade, arriving at precisely 11 o'clock. There she takes the royal salute from the Household Division – her own personal troops – and inspects the various Foot Guards regiments. As a younger woman, the Queen carried out the inspection from the saddle of her own horse, but in recent decades this accomplished equestrian has chosen instead to conduct proceedings from the comfort of a state coach.

Each year, a different Foot Guards regiment is chosen to parade, or troop, its colours through the ranks of the other regiments. This done, the entire Household Division, more than 1,000 officers and men, march past the Queen, saluting as they go and marching – or, in the case of the cavalry, walking – to the sound of the massed bands of the Foot Guards, the mounted bands of the Household Cavalry and a Corps of Drums to boot. Amounting to more than 400 musicians, the whole ensemble can make a substantial noise even outdoors. When the ceremony is over, the royal party returns to Buckingham Palace to receive a 41-gun salute fired from nearby Green Park, before making their way onto the balcony of the palace to watch a fly-past by the Royal Air Force.

PRIDE IN LONDON

Pride in London, which takes place every year on a weekend in high summer around the end of June, is one of the biggest LGBT festivals in Europe. It grew out of the Gay Pride political rallies of the early 1970s, which began as a response to the Stonewall Riots in the USA in 1969, and in the wake of the decriminalisation of homosexuality in the UK two years earlier. Since then, Pride has grown to become an annual event attracting hundreds of thousands of gay, lesbian, bisexual and transgender people, as well as heterosexuals who like a good party. The centrepiece is a march with a huge rainbow flag: through London's West End, from the western end of Oxford Street to Oxford Circus, and then down Regent Street to Piccadilly Circus, ending in Trafalgar Square, where since

2004 a political rally has been held, continuing the tradition of the early events. In 2014, some 30,000 people took part in the march.

WIMBLEDON CHAMPIONSHIPS

The Wimbledon Tennis Championships occur every summer at the All England Club in Wimbledon, southwest London, in the last week of June and first week of July. The first championships were held in 1877, making Wimbledon the oldest and most famous tennis tournament in the world, as well as the most prestigious of the four Grand Slams. It is also the only one of the Slams still played on grass. Wimbledon has two show courts but its schedule has at times been vulnerable to capricious British weather. So in 2009 a fully retractable roof was added to the principal court, known as Centre Court.

The first tournament to be televised was in 1937, the year after the British player Fred Perry won his third and final title. Although there have been several British winners of the women's title over the years, the last being Virginia Wade in 1977, it was not until 2013 that Andy Murray became the next British winner of the men's title after Perry. In between, Wimbledon has seen the greatest players in the history of the game – from Björn Borg to Pete Sampras to Roger Federer, and from Martina Navratilova to Steffi Graf to Serena Williams – play some of the greatest matches in history on the hallowed grass of Centre Court.

TEST CRICKET AT LORD'S

Unlike football – a British invention taken up with gusto by people in countries outside the British sphere of influence – cricket remains a ruling passion for many nations that were once part of the British Empire and a byzantine mystery to those that were not. To lovers of the game, Lord's is the home of cricket. The original ground established by Thomas Lord in 1787 was on the site of Dorset Square, close to Marylebone Station. The current Lord's Cricket Ground was established in 1814 on a site a little further north in St John's Wood, north London.

Lord's is officially the home of the Marylebone Cricket Club, or MCC, but it is also the leading international venue in the cricketing world. However, despite its seminal role in the game, the ground was not the site of the first-ever Test match, which instead took place in Melbourne, Australia, in 1877 – needless to say, Australia won the contest by 45 runs! In fact, it was not until 1884 that Lord's staged its first Test match, again involving the only two Test-playing nations of the time; since then more than 100 Tests have been played there. The Lord's Test has always been an eagerly awaited event: the principal fixture in any cricketing summer. But these days the demands of television deals and the increased number of teams that play Test cricket – there are now ten in all – mean there are Test series against two separate teams each summer, with a Test at the home of cricket in each series.

Lord's today is a typical London mixture of old and modern. The stately Victorian pavilion still dominates the ground, with the players' access to the pitch still requiring that they walk through the famous Long Room, where a doting honour guard of MCC members claps them onto the field. But the ground was substantially renovated at the end of the twentieth century, with the addition of new stands and the spaceship-like Media Centre. However, the mystique of Lord's for cricket fans is its history, and this can be explored in the MCC Museum at the ground. Among its artefacts is the little terracotta urn commemorating what to the English was an infamous sporting calamity. In 1882 at the Kennington Oval, London's other international cricket ground, the touring Australian team thrashed the home side. Such was the humiliation felt by the English at being so humbled by the colonial team in the imperial capital that a pair of bails from one of the wickets was burned and the ashes placed symbolically in the frail little casket, representing the incineration of English cricketing hope. Ever since, the England and Australia teams have contested a series known as the Ashes.

NOTTING HILL CARNIVAL

The Notting Hill Carnival, which happens every year over the last weekend in August, has been a fixture in the London calendar since 1964. It began as a local celebration of West Indian culture and a way of promoting social harmony in a part of West London where immigrants from the Caribbean had settled over the previous two decades; previous years had seen attacks against black people, culminating most notoriously in the Notting Hill riots of 1958. Partly because of this history, it has since become a festival that Londoners of all backgrounds now embrace as their own. It has also grown into a major global event, attracting one million visitors annually, making it the biggest street party in Europe.

The Carnival is renowned for the colourful, flamboyant costumes made every year by legions of volunteers and for the gentle, lilting steel-band music, originating from the Caribbean, which ripples through the streets. On the first day, the Family Day or Sunday Parade, some 50,000 participants – musicians and dancers – swing through the neighbourhoods of Notting Hill and the surrounding areas of Ladbroke Grove, Westbourne Grove, Westbourne Park and Kensal Road. The second day, the Grand Finale, sees streets overflow with steel bands and mobile sound systems pumping out everything from reggae to dubstep, as well as the dancers in their fabulous costumes enjoying their moment in the sun – or, this being Britain, possibly rain. There are also countless stalls selling Caribbean street food. All in all, it is one big jamboree and, as such, continues the devil-may-care spirit of old London events like Bartholomew Fair.

PEARLY KINGS AND QUEENS HARVEST FESTIVAL

Every year at the start of autumn, the Pearly Kings and Queens celebrate their harvest festival by parading the short distance through the City of London from Guildhall Yard to the church of St Mary-le-Bow. The distinctive attire of the Pearlies, as they are known, is one of London's most characteristic sights, familiar to people around the world thanks to their appearance in Walt Disney's film *Mary Poppins* (1964) and, most recently, the part they played in the opening ceremony parade of the 2012 London Olympic Games.

The Pearlies were started in 1875 by Henry Croft, a young lad raised in an orphanage in Somers Town in northwest London. He started work, at the age of 13, as a sweeper in the local market, where he was struck by the kindness of the market traders, known as costermongers, who cared for and looked after each other when one or another fell sick. He was also very taken with the mother-of-pearl buttons they sewed to the seams of their trousers. Determined that he would follow their charitable example, the young lad began collecting up the pearl buttons he found around the market and sewing them to his own clothes to draw attention to himself. Soon he had covered his cap with them and before long an entire suit, known as a smother suit, was also covered in buttons. Still today it is the men, the Pearly Kings, rather than the Queens, who do all the designs and all the sewing.

Henry's example proved an inspiration to others, and soon many of his friends among the costermongers had become the first Pearly families, whose descendants today still adhere to the original tradition, which Henry established more than a century ago, of raising money for charity. Each of its 30 'royal families' is associated with a different church in central London, as well as a different borough of the wider city. A marble statue of Henry Croft can be seen today in the crypt of that most charitable of London's churches, St Martin-in-the-Fields.

TUDOR LONDON

Like the rest of the country, and indeed Europe, it took London a long time to recover from the Black Death and the pandemics, some almost as devastating, which beset the city between 1350 and 1550. By 1450, a century after the most deadly plague, the population of London had recovered only slightly, to 50,000 people, but the range of traded goods had expanded by 1500 to include tennis balls, liquorice, Bruges silk, warming pans, thimbles, paper and dye for cloth.

Above all, Britain was growing rich on the wool trade, to the extent that in 1540 wool accounted for some 88 per cent of all English exports. In that context, the traditional right extended to any freeman of the City of London to drive his sheep across London Bridge seems slightly less eccentric, considering that 500 years ago possession of a flock meant access to a fortune. Close to half of the City's freemen in the early sixteenth century were members of cloth-related guilds, while of the 80 different people to hold the office of Lord Mayor between 1485 and 1558, 45 had made their fortunes in the cloth trade. In 1559, the year after Elizabeth I took the throne, one William Hewett, a Yorkshire cloth worker who had prospered since coming to London, was made the first Protestant Lord Mayor of the City, confirming the ascendancy of the new religion under the Virgin Queen.

By this point most of London's great abbeys had been destroyed in the purge of Catholicism that happened following Henry VIII's divorce from the Church of Rome. But despite the cultural schism with the rest of Europe, in the late sixteenth century London became a world city and England, increasingly, a global power with a navy and an appetite for exploration that rivalled the more established fleets of Portugal and Spain. London's population had more than quadrupled by 1605 to some 225,000 – one-sixth of the population of England, an even higher proportion than today – in spite of the loss of 30,000 lives to yet another outbreak of plague only two years earlier, the year Queen Bess herself had died.

This expansion was mirrored in the cultural flowering known as the English Renaissance, when some of England's greatest houses and palaces, some of its most impressive music and some of its finest poetry emerged from the capital. Pre-eminent among the figures of this golden age is William Shakespeare, whose plays stand as the keystone of all literature in the English language and, of course, were first performed in London's Globe Theatre. Other great playwrights of the age – in particular, Ben Jonson and Christopher Marlowe – staged works at the various rival theatres that grew up along the South Bank during the last quarter of the sixteenth century.

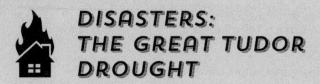

DISASTERS: THE GREAT TUDOR DROUGHT

The Tudor period may have been a golden age, but the Tudors were even more vulnerable to climate fluctuations than we are today. From February 1540 to October the following year, Europe experienced the most prolonged drought in its history. Rivers dried up – even major ones like the Seine and the Rhine – and parts of the Continent turned to desert, with even forests in Britain beginning to die on account of the heat. March and April 1540 were hot, but the summer was blistering. In London, between February and September 1540, it rained a mere six times, causing the freshwater Thames to dwindle to such an extent that incoming tidal seawater was able to flow through the close-set piers of London Bridge and into the freshwater wells that fed the city. The polluted water supplies caused an outbreak of cholera and dysentery that killed thousands. When the rain finally did arrive in October 1541, it persisted to such an extent that there was widespread flooding the following year.

ALONG THE RIVER: HAMMERSMITH BRIDGE TO ALBERT BRIDGE

As we drift downstream from Hammersmith Bridge, we pass the London Wetland Centre on our right and Craven Cottage, the home of Fulham Football Club, on our left. A little further along, also on the river's north bank, is **Fulham Palace**, once the residence of the Bishops of London and today a series of buildings with a range of architectural styles from the Tudor to the Victorian era.

Under Putney Bridge and Wandsworth Bridge, and after numerous small parks on both sides of the river, eventually we come to Albert Bridge, which – along with Hammersmith Bridge – is one of the most elegant in London. Designed and built in 1873 as a cable-stayed bridge, it proved to be so unstable that a decade later Sir Joseph Bazalgette, who had already redesigned Hammersmith Bridge, was called on again to put it on a firmer footing, which he did by introducing elements of a suspension bridge. However, as was the case with Hammersmith, the growth in weight of traffic led the Greater London Council in 1973 to add two concrete piers to support the centre of the bridge. The resulting hybrid sounds like a mess but is in fact rather graceful, especially at night, when the structure is illuminated by some 4,000 lights and becomes one of the city's most charming sights.

BUILDING LONDON

London's longevity is the key to its urban character. Perhaps more than in any other major world city, internationally significant buildings from 1,000 years of history (and some remnants almost 1,000 years older than that) have survived amid bold contemporary architecture. An older neighbourhood is sometimes given a bit of architectural Viagra with the addition of a striking new building or two, as has happened in the City in recent years; or an older institution is given a stunning extension, as in the case of St Pancras International station or the 1930s addition to medieval **Eltham Palace** in southeast London, whose spacious atrium has probably the finest Art Deco interior in the UK. In the same way, an old building is transformed from a derelict has-been into a repurposed trendsetter, as was the case when the former Bankside Power Station became Tate Modern.

Some of these examples make appearances in other sections of the book, but here are highlighted some of London's most distinctive architectural icons, which collectively demonstrate the mix of tradition and innovation that reflect the values of the city and its people. The process of gentrification, with run-down neighbourhoods becoming hip, has its downsides, as countless Londoners struggle to get by in what is now one of the most expensive cities on Earth, with many new housing developments aimed at incomes far beyond those of the people who make the capital tick. This is a problem transforming communities all over London, one with no easy solution. But while many icons of past and present seem to be the grandest buildings – royal residences such as Buckingham Palace or symbols of commerce like the Shard – in fact, some of London's most astonishing spaces, such as the extraordinary interior of 575 Wandsworth Road, are among the most humble: a reminder that any building owes its particular quality not just to the design but to the people who have lived in it and loved it over many years.

TOWER OF LONDON

The Tower of London in the British imagination evokes grim scenes of summary judgment, imprisonment and death. In the Middle Ages and in Tudor times it was a common fate for enemies of the realm to be 'sent to the Tower', as the phrase has it, to await execution or, in some cases, some even more ignominious demise. Most notoriously, the two young sons of Edward IV, known as the Princes in the Tower, were probably held and assassinated there in 1483, on the orders of their uncle Richard, Duke of Gloucester, who would be next in line to the throne once the two boys were out of the way.

In fact, though it saw much use as a prison, particularly in the sixteenth and seventeenth centuries, very few people were executed in the Tower itself (the deed was usually done on nearby Tower Hill); for example, during the two world wars of the twentieth century a number of enemy spies did meet that fate on the site by order of the British Government. Two of the final cohort of prisoners to be held there were the infamous Kray twins, Ronnie and Reggie, who in 1952 assaulted a police officer after going absent without leave from National Service. Later released from another prison, they went on to do far worse things as kings of London's criminal underworld in the 1960s.

But the Tower was always intended as a palace, albeit an increasingly well-fortified one in the defensive tradition of the Middle Ages. The current ensemble of buildings and sturdy curtain walls took shape over more than two centuries after the Norman Conquest of 1066. The White Tower – to give the central building of the complex its proper name – was built in 1078 on the orders of William of Normandy himself as a statement of his authority, its mighty keep dominating the cityscape of late Saxon London.

Further buildings and defences were added during the reigns of Richard I in the 1190s (the Inner Ward) and Edward I almost a century later (the Outer Ward). It was in the green sward beyond the outer wall that in 2014 British artists Paul Cummins and Tom Piper created one of the most memorable public spectacles London has ever seen when they filled this now-dry moat with 888,246 ceramic poppies to commemorate each of the British or

Colonial servicemen and women believed to have died in World War One. The installation attracted millions of visitors through its four-month run, but even in an ordinary year the Tower is one of London's most visited attractions: a UNESCO World Heritage Site, where tourists come to see the Crown Jewels, the famous Yeoman Warders in their distinctive uniforms, or the ravens, looked after by the Warders to keep them at the Tower. Legend has it that if these talismanic birds should ever leave, the monarchy will fall.

HAMPTON COURT PALACE

Hampton Court Palace is not one palace but two. Situated on the non-tidal Thames above Teddington Lock, on the outer edge of today's southwest London (though far from the city at the time), it was originally the brainchild of Cardinal Thomas Wolsey, chief minister to the young King Henry VIII, who in 1514 took over the site and began to develop what he intended would be the finest palace in England. Indeed, the Tudor façade is still what greets visitors approaching the main entrance today. Beyond this is a courtyard, the Base Court, with an astronomical clock that is still functioning set into the brickwork above another gate at the far side.

In 1528, Wolsey, feeling increasingly out of favour with the king, made the magnanimous gesture of giving the palace to Henry. Thus, the inner gate is known as Anne Boleyn's Gate, as the apartments above it were designed for the use of Henry's second wife, though, alas, the king tired of her and had her beheaded before she could get to enjoy them. By this time the Great Hall had been added – with its high, hammerbeam ceiling – as well as the Royal Tennis Court, where even today visitors to the palace can sometimes see competitors playing a set of real tennis, the precursor to the modern game.

After Henry's reign, the palace was less favoured by subsequent monarchs, with Elizabeth preferring the now almost vanished Richmond Palace further downriver. Indeed, Hampton Court became only an occasional residence for the Stuart kings, its architectural style by then seen as rather outmoded. It took a Dutchman to see the potential of Hampton Court once again: the Protestant William of Orange, who in 1688 removed the Catholic King James II from the English throne in a bloodless coup known as the Glorious Revolution. William's alterations resulted in the demolition of half the original Tudor structure, which would have been a more lamentable loss if what replaced it – new royal apartments built of red brick to harmonise with the earlier palace – had not been designed by Sir Christopher Wren, then at the absolute zenith of his fame. Intended as a Baroque palace to rival Versailles, the apartments that were built are in fact only a part of the planned scheme, as William lost interest in the project following the death of Queen Mary, his wife and co-monarch, in 1694.

As a result, today's palace is a stimulating contrast of two periods of architecture and two eras of English history. The impressive gardens and grounds, on the other hand, all date from William's remodelling, including the Hampton Court

Maze. Today the gardens are the annual site for the Hampton Court Flower Show.

BANQUETING HOUSE

Banqueting House is the only surviving building from the huge Palace of Whitehall close to Westminster Abbey, another of Henry VIII's palaces which had previously belonged to Cardinal Wolsey. Henry had the complex of buildings extended to become what was then the largest palace in Europe. The present building was constructed in the early 1620s during the reign of James I. Designed by Inigo Jones, who was strongly influenced by the Italian Renaissance example of Andrea Palladio, Banqueting House was a radical break with tradition: one of the first Neoclassical buildings in England (along with Jones's Queen's House in Greenwich) and, as such, a seminal example of the architectural character which London would acquire over the next three centuries.

After King James's death, Banqueting House quickly became the favoured residence of his son, Charles I. During the first decade of his reign, he enjoyed masques there – theatrical entertainments involving words, music, dance, and lavish sets and costumes – staged on winter nights in the grand hall on the upper floor, lit by flaming torches and coloured lamps that lent to proceedings an atmosphere of mystery and magic. Charles, among all British kings, was also the greatest lover of fine art, so the smoke-filled masques were moved to another hall when in 1636 nine ceiling murals commissioned from Peter Paul Rubens were fixed in place. They are still there today – the only such Rubens scheme anywhere in Europe to remain in its original position.

Charles was forced to abandon the palace during the English Civil War of the 1640s but, in a spiteful twist of fate, in 1649 it became his place of execution. On a cold January morning, the deposed monarch is led through an upstairs window onto a temporary scaffold, where a crowd was eagerly waiting for the axe to fall. Almost 50 years later, in 1698, the Palace of Whitehall burnt to the ground, with only Banqueting House surviving the inferno. It stands today not only as a memorial to past magnificence but as a reminder of the only regicide in English history.

OLD ROYAL NAVAL COLLEGE

The Old Royal Naval College in Greenwich, formerly the Greenwich Hospital, is perhaps the greatest Wren masterpiece of all. Along with other historic buildings in Greenwich, it forms one of London's four UNESCO World Heritage Sites, and was described by the cultural organisation as the 'finest and most dramatically sited architectural and landscape ensemble in the British Isles'. It is hard to disagree as you approach the sublime symmetry created by the split ensemble of buildings, especially from the river, with their two small domes echoing the Cathedral of St Paul's, which was still under construction when work began on the Greenwich site in 1694. In fact, this twinned solution – where the two sides are mirrors of each other, as if reflected in water – was forced upon the architect by Queen Mary, who had commissioned the Royal Hospital for Seamen, as it was officially known, in response to the suffering of sailors returning from war. The two sides frame a view to the **Queen's House**, the Neoclassical villa by Inigo Jones, which has recently been refurbished.

Queen Mary had insisted that the architect create a central avenue so that views from the house to the river would not be blocked. Beneath the two domes are a chapel on the east side and, on the west, the magnificent Painted Hall, whose muralled ceilings created over a period of two decades by Sir James Thornhill honour a succession of contemporary Protestant monarchs from William and Mary, through Queen Anne to King George I. After the hospital closed in 1873, ownership of the buildings passed to the Royal Navy, whose college in the premises closed as recently as 1998. The buildings have enjoyed a range of tenants and uses since then, though both Chapel and Painted Hall are open to the public.

CHISWICK HOUSE

Chiswick House was the first neo-Palladian villa in London and is regarded as the finest surviving example in the city. Designed by Richard Boyle, the 3rd Earl of Burlington, and completed in 1729, the house was intended to recreate the style of villas he had seen on his travels on the Grand Tour – such as Palladio's 'La Rotonda' near Vicenza, in northern Italy, with its similar symmetrical arrangement of rooms around a central Domed Hall.

The muralled and decorated interiors on the upper floor were created over a long period by Lord Burlington's friend, William Kent. It was the latter who helped to create the gardens, which if anything were even more influential than the house and are now regarded as a main inspiration for the English Landscape Movement that emerged during the later eighteenth century. Inspired by ideas about the garden tastes of Ancient Rome, they are filled with classical statues – free-standing or perched on top of columns, some genuine and some fake – as well as miniature temples, obelisks, funerary urns and other classical paraphernalia.

BUCKINGHAM PALACE

Buckingham Palace was not always as grand as it is today. When George III took the throne in 1760, marrying the following year, the existing centre of court, St James's Palace, was not a comfortable place to bring up a young family, so his advisors secured for him a modest stately home known as Buckingham House. Over time, it seemed insufficiently grand so in 1821, the year after George's son and successor took the throne as George IV, the new king instructed his friend and architect John Nash to remodel and extend the palace – additions which also included two whole new wings.

When Nash was dismissed upon the death of George IV, work on the palace remained unfinished, and even in the mid-1840s, some years into her reign, Queen Victoria would complain of having nowhere big enough to accommodate her growing family and the numerous people she was expected to receive. So in 1847 the east wing was built, fully enclosing the existing three-sided forecourt, and the palace was redecorated with lavish modern elegance. Victoria's son and successor, Edward VII, was responsible for the **Victoria Memorial** which stands in the middle of the roundabout in front of the main gates, and then in 1913, during the reign of his brother George V, the final part was added: the new façade of Portland Stone that is now the world-famous image of the palace.

Since 1993, the impressive state rooms have been opened to the public for a limited period every summer while the Queen is on her summer break. Visitors can see where so many heads of state have been entertained during the six and a half decades of the present monarch's reign and they can also view the Old Master paintings, one of the finest private collections in the world.

Behind the house is an extensive garden backing onto Green Park, where every summer the Queen hosts her famous garden parties. Out front, approaching 11 o'clock every morning (and on alternate days in the colder months), crowds gather to watch the Changing of the Guard, one of the many public rituals that paint London as a place of traditions, which over many centuries appear not to have changed at all.

BOUNDARY ESTATE

In fact, London changed considerably during the nineteenth century, and by the end of Victoria's reign, the population of some six million people was more than three times what it had been at the start. As a result, in the 1890s large areas of the capital, and particularly the East End, were chronically overcrowded, with disease and malnutrition leading to high infant mortality and low life expectancy for those who survived into adulthood. The worst of the slums was Old Nichol in Bethnal Green, and in 1894 the then London County Council hit upon a radical plan. The resident population was moved out, the old low-rise terraces were demolished and in their place a new development – the first publicly funded housing estate in London – was built. The new five storey apartment blocks, which formed the Boundary Estate and were strongly influenced by the Arts and Crafts Movement, were clustered along seven streets radiating out from a central communal space, Arnold Circus, whose raised central mound was topped by a bandstand which is still there today.

When it opened in 1900, the estate greatly increased the available housing stock in the area, though many of its former tenants could not afford to move back there because of the higher rents; gentrification is not a new phenomenon. But unlike so many similar, later developments in London, the Boundary Estate today is still providing social housing to residents of the two boroughs of Hackney and Tower Hamlets, whose common boundary it bestrides.

HIGHPOINT I

Highpoint I, in Highgate, is well named. Designed by the Russian-born architect, Berthold Lubetkin, and built in 1935 on one of the capital's highest plots of land, this residential block of 64 flats was one of the first modernist buildings in London and is regarded as a classic of the International Style, earning praise from Le Corbusier himself. It was originally commissioned by Sigmund Gestetner to provide social housing for workers of his office equipment firm, but when middle-class buyers saw plans for this futuristic development on a superb site overlooking the city, the two- and three-bedroom apartments were soon snapped up. A second, more luxurious, development – Highpoint II – was built in 1938 on a neighbouring site, and both structures are now Grade I listed buildings.

ALEXANDRA ROAD ESTATE

The Alexandra Road Estate at the northern end of Abbey Road, on the southern boundary of the borough of Camden, is a classic of Brutalist architecture. Built in a graceful arc dictated by the curve of an adjacent railway line, this visionary housing development designed in 1968 by Neave Brown, an architect with Camden Council, was not completed until a decade later. It consists of three crescent-shaped apartment blocks designed in the form of ziggurats so as to let in more light to what is in fact a high-density site. The higher, eight-storey block backs onto the railway line and the ziggurat projects in cantilevered form across the tracks, apparently shielding the estate from the noise of the trains. It is no surprise that this remarkable location has featured in numerous films and television programmes: walking along the pedestrian street that curves between the two most northerly blocks feels like strolling through a futuristic film set.

575 WANDSWORTH ROAD

This unremarkable Georgian terraced house was bought in 1981, in a state of considerable disrepair, by Khadambi Asalache, because the no. 77 bus ran from right outside his door to his place of work at HM Treasury in Whitehall. A polymath who had completed an MPhil in the philosophy of mathematics before assuming his civil service post, Khadambi, as the guides in the house refer to him, was already a published poet and novelist, one of his native Kenya's most significant literary figures. But his greatest work was ahead of him, as quietly he set about transforming the house's interior into an environment that properly reflected the copious riches of a well-stocked mind.

Summoning many influences, but principally the Moorish architecture of Andalusia, the decorated doorways of Zanzibar, the panelled interiors of Damascus and the waterside houses of Istanbul, Khadambi took old Victorian floorboards and other bits of wood he found in skips around the area and painstakingly cut them into the delicate fretwork panels that today adorn the walls throughout the house. But the cultural range of the decoration goes way beyond the obvious Islamic influences and is impossible to summarise, except to say that when walking around the house, there is no culture you would not expect to see referenced in Khadambi's endlessly various decorative schemes.

Khadambi died in 2006, by which time he had agreed to leave this multicultural masterpiece of decorative art to the National Trust. It is truly a marvel of modern London.

THE LLOYD'S BUILDING

Situated in the heart of the City, this is one building that could be said to symbolise the resurgence of the capital over the past 30 years. Lloyd's of London is one of the City's most enduring institutions: an international insurance market more than 300 years old, which since 1871 has been governed by its own Act of Parliament. Designed by Richard Rogers, now Lord Rogers, the new Lloyd's Building opened in 1986, the same year in which Prime Minister Margaret Thatcher deregulated the financial markets – a liberalising move known as Big Bang, which brought great benefits to some but whose drawbacks have become increasingly apparent since the crash of 2008.

Rogers's avant-garde building seemed to embody the new lightly regulated, risk-taking atmosphere of the Square Mile in the age of the yuppie. Deploying a similar set of ideas to the plan which had worked so successfully on the Pompidou Centre in Paris the Lloyd's Building places all its services – all the pipes and ducts, staircases, glass lifts, fire escapes and even toilet pods – on the outside of the building. This makes for a complex façade that is hard to comprehend but still fascinating to behold. If it has recently been put somewhat in the shade (quite literally) by the newer, even bigger, buildings that now surround it, the Lloyd's Building was profoundly radical in its day, sticking up like a sore thumb (or perhaps a shiny, misshapen thimble) beside the Neoclassical buildings that the financial bastions of the City had traditionally occupied – such as the **Royal Exchange** at Bank. Once a home to Lloyd's itself for a period of 150 years, this is now, tellingly, a luxury development of upmarket dining and retail.

ST PANCRAS INTERNATIONAL STATION

The breathtaking new St Pancras International station is the redevelopment of the old St Pancras railway station into a domestic and international terminus serving destinations in the East Midlands and parts of the Southeast of England, as well as Continental Europe via the Eurostar line. Developed by Alastair Lansley from a masterplan by Norman Foster, now Lord Foster, it opened in 2007 and is regularly voted among the world's favourite stations.

When the old rail shed designed by William Henry Barlow opened in the 1860s, it had the largest single-span roof in the world. The Foster scheme significantly expanded and reconfigured the station, so that trains now arrive beneath the new extension, in four different sections, while the old shed encloses a retail space and a wide public concourse, complete with rickety second-hand pianos which any member of the public can play if a spot of busking tickles their fancy.

Adjoining the original station was the **Midland Grand Hotel**, designed by Sir George Gilbert Scott and opened in 1873 – a classic piece of mid-Victorian Gothic architecture. This had closed in 1935 and was then used as railway offices until the 1980s, after which it lay empty for many years. But the redevelopment of the station revived interest in this grand Victorian pile, which reopened in 2011 as a five-star hotel, beneath the 68 new luxury apartments created on the building's upper floors.

SEVENTEENTH-CENTURY LONDON: A TIME OF TURMOIL

The seventeenth century was the most turbulent in English history and some of the most significant events involved the Westminster Parliament in London, its relationship with the monarchy and the issue of religion. This turmoil began in 1605 with the Gunpowder Plot, in which a group of Catholic dissidents attempted to blow up Parliament when the King was also present. The plot was foiled, the plotters were executed and King James died a natural death, but his son and successor, Charles I, would not be so lucky. Believing in the divine right of kings, throughout the 1630s he continually dissolved Parliament by royal diktat when it did not accede to his demands. Things came to a head in 1642 when the King entered the House of Commons without consent and attempted to arrest five MPs on grounds of treason. The accused members were not present, forewarned of the King's plan, but the remainder were so incensed that Charles was forced to quit his palace in nearby Whitehall and flee the capital in fear for his safety. Seven years later, at the end of a terrible civil war – the only one in England's history – Charles, now defeated and deposed, was back in London, where on 30 January he succumbed to the executioner's blade.

London had backed Parliament against the King at an early stage in that conflict, and in 1642 the Parliamentary forces had turned back the King's army at Turnham Green in today's West London. Following the death of Charles, in 1653 Oliver Cromwell became Lord Protector of England's first and only republic. This constitutional experiment would be short-lived. After Cromwell himself had dissolved Parliament on more than one occasion, having once led the army that sought to defend it, the monarchy was restored in 1660. The subsequent reign of King Charles II, a period known as the Restoration, has been caricatured as one of hedonistic indulgence, dominated by an atmosphere of frivolity embodied in the principal theatrical entertainment during this period: the Restoration comedy. These often licentious plays, staged in new London theatres in Dorset Gardens and Drury Lane, were written not only by men such as John Dryden and William Wycherley, but also in later years by Aphra Behn, a pioneer among female playwrights in English. For the first time they also featured female actors; one of these, Nell Gwyn, became the most famous of the King's many mistresses and the pair had an illegitimate son.

For London, however, the most significant events of the period, occurring in consecutive years, were not political or cultural, but natural. Although together they brought the city to its knees, its response to these catastrophes, arguably the worst the capital has known, would put a stamp on London which has defined its character ever since.

DISASTERS: THE GREAT PLAGUE AND THE GREAT FIRE

At the end of 1664 the area around Drury Lane saw the first cases in the last and most notorious of the many major plague epidemics to have afflicted the capital throughout its history. London was still a filthy, rat-infested city with abysmal sanitation and regular, virulent outbreaks of disease. The Great Plague which ravaged the city in 1665 took a toll of perhaps as many as 100,000 people – almost a quarter of the populace – and is compellingly recorded in Daniel Defoe's *A Journal of the Plague Year* (1722), a fictional account written more than 50 years later that reads like eyewitness reportage.

But the event which has overshadowed this calamity, almost as if buildings somehow mattered more than people, occurred a matter of months after the last death from the plague. The Great Fire of London, which young children still learn about today in the popular round 'London's Burning', started on the night of 2 September 1666 in the bakery of the king's own baker, Mr Farriner, on Pudding Lane next to London Bridge, a site commemorated soon afterwards by the **Monument**: the memorial column which can still be climbed internally to reach a viewing platform at the top. The death toll from the fire was in fact minuscule – perhaps as few as six people lost their lives in a conflagration that lasted three days – yet the trauma to the city was colossal. The fire was eventually put out when firebreaks were created where houses that stood in the path of the inferno were blown up to prevent it spreading. But by then some 60 per cent of the buildings within a vast area inside the city wall – the medieval city depicted in the *Long View of London*, Wenceslaus Hollar's classic 5 metre-long panorama from 1647 – had been completely razed to the ground. In all, from the Tower of London in the east to the Temple in the west, more than 13,000 houses, 87 churches, 44 out of 47 guild halls and even old St Paul's Cathedral went up in the blaze, with more than 70,000 people displaced. Looking down on the devastation from 'Barking steeple' (All Hallows by the Tower), Samuel Pepys described it in his famous diary as 'the saddest sight of desolation that I ever saw; every where great fires, oyle-cellars, and brimstone, and other things burning'.

However, in a classic demonstration of resilience, within weeks the task of reconstructing the city had been handed to the architect whose great London buildings are still some of its most instantly recognisable icons. In fact, Sir Christopher Wren's masterplan for the rebuilt city, involving wide boulevards and a much more rational distribution of streets, was never enacted, as land and property owners asserted their rights and new buildings were put up on the existing plots following the same rabbit warren of streets as before. But if Wren the master-planner was thwarted, over the next three decades Wren the architect was able to exercise the full range of his gifts, redesigning and rebuilding many of the destroyed medieval churches in astounding architectural variety, and living long enough to see the completion of the new St Paul's Cathedral.

ALONG THE RIVER: ALBERT BRIDGE TO BATTERSEA POWER STATION

From Albert Bridge we continue towards Chelsea Bridge, passing Battersea Park, whose most unusual feature can be seen from the river. The Peace Pagoda was completed in 1985 by the Reverend Gyoro Nagase, a Japanese Buddhist monk, and some 50 volunteers, and is now a much-loved landmark for people who use the park. Just under Chelsea Bridge and then Grosvenor Bridge, which carries trains into and out of Victoria Station, we come to another building whose quartet of chimney stacks is beloved both by Londoners and by many from all over the world who are familiar with London's more contemporary landmarks.

Battersea Power Station, one of the largest brick buildings in the world, has a monumental presence suggesting great age, but in fact the first of the two power stations that would make up this Art Deco 'temple of power', as it was once described, only became operational in 1934. Designed by Sir Giles Gilbert Scott, its time as a working power station ended on 31 October 1983 – a period of less than 50 years – when the second of the two stations shut down for good. Numerous plans have been drawn up to adapt this colossus into a viable post-industrial space, but none has come to fruition, while the fabric of the building has become increasingly fragile.

But the latest plan seems destined to succeed, with a scheduled reopening in 2020 as a mix of high-end retail, residential units and leisure space, as well as businesses as high-profile as Apple pledging to relocate some of their offices there.

COLLECTING
LONDON

Even if we set aside its art galleries for another part of the book, London has one of the richest and most diverse ranges of major museums in the world, a legacy of the curiosity and determination – and in some cases the opportunism – of the generations of British explorers, scientists, antiquarians, colonial officials and others who are responsible for the capital's great collections. But if the city's most august institutions are rightly world-renowned, some of the most surprising and most accessible collections can be found in lesser-known museums such as Sir John Soane's Museum or the **Horniman Museum** in Forest Hill, southeast London, with its superb display of musical instruments from around the world and possibly the best collection of African artefacts anywhere in the UK. It is in such smaller places that we can sense the voracious curiosity of London's great collectors. Indeed, major museums like the British Museum and the Natural History Museum had similar small beginnings, which over time became the wonderful collections that today draw visitors from across the globe.

THE BRITISH MUSEUM

The British Museum is the most visited museum in London and among the most visited in the world, with nearly seven million people coming through its doors in 2015. It's little wonder, as there are only a tiny handful of places anywhere that hold so many artefacts and art objects from the entirety of human history. The museum is one of the oldest such institutions, first established in 1753 from the private collection that Sir Hans Sloane – a royal physician, naturalist and collector – bequeathed to the nation upon his death.

Sloane's collection was gradually added to, with the first important antiquities – a collection of Greek vases – being acquired in 1772. Thereafter, the expansion of the British Empire saw new and wondrous treasures brought back by explorers and victorious military commanders from all corners of the globe, beginning in the early nineteenth century with objects from Egypt and Greece such as the code-breaking Rosetta Stone and the now controversial Parthenon Marbles.

Otherwise known as the Elgin Marbles after the peer of the realm who, according to some historians, bribed officials in Ottoman Athens to let him remove them from the Acropolis, these sculpted reliefs are among the museum's most important objects. While the Greek government is adamant that these friezes are the property of the Greek people and should be returned, the British Museum insists on the legality of Elgin's original purchase. With recent events in Syria and Iraq, where irreplaceable antiquities have been desecrated beyond repair, another side of the debate suggests that great museums of world culture based in relatively stable regions have a universal function to look after the inheritance of all humanity. Extraordinary works of art in the museum's collection, such as the Assyrian Lion Hunt reliefs, might not exist at all now if they had been left in or returned to their place of origin, though a single glance at history would make a sensible person hesitate before declaring any region to be stable in the long term. That is one of the lessons a great museum like this one teaches us.

The museum's current Neoclassical building, designed by Sir Robert Smirke to accommodate a collection that was being steadily enlarged by the institution's own expeditions overseas, was completed in 1857 but within half a century was expanding once again, as more precious antiquities were added, such as the exquisite Aztec turquoise double-headed serpent or the extensive grave goods from the Anglo-Saxon ship burial discovered at Sutton Hoo in 1939. Then in the last decade of the twentieth century the British Library moved out of its long-standing home in the museum's quadrangle, the old circular Reading Room was converted into a temporary exhibition space and the entire courtyard – the Great Court, as it is known – was enclosed by a gridshell glass roof designed by the practice of Lord Foster. This was high enough to accommodate two magnificent giant totem poles from the Haida culture of British Columbia, which still stand in the Great Court today.

NATURAL HISTORY MUSEUM

The greater part of Sir Hans Sloane's collection comprised specimens of flora and fauna which for more than a century were a mere department within the British Museum, but in time formed the principal holdings of the Natural History Museum on Exhibition Road in South Kensington – London's street of museums, named for the Great Exhibition of 1851 which took place in nearby Hyde Park. The gigantic neo-Romanesque building was designed by Alfred Waterhouse and opened to the public in 1881. Since 1986, it has incorporated the Geological Museum in its collections, so that the museum's total collection of life and earth sciences specimens now runs to around 80 million items. Some of the zoological collection – namely, the millions of preserved specimens – is now housed in the Darwin Centre, which opened in 2002.

The star exhibits start with a suspended blue whale skeleton in the main hall and include several complete dinosaur skeletons of such perennial favourites as Stegosaurus and Triceratops. Another reliable wow is the Large Mammals Hall, which still features the same collection of stuffed land and aquatic mammals – including the giant model of a blue whale that has been there since 1938 – which anyone who has ever visited the museum will remember. The Treasures Gallery contains some of the finest specimens in the collection or those with particular historical significance, such as: a wonderful fossil of an archaeopteryx – long established as the missing link between dinosaurs and birds – the skeleton of a dodo, the pigeons (now stuffed) which helped Darwin develop his theory of evolution by natural selection and an Emperor penguin egg collected by Captain Scott on his fateful expedition to Antarctica in 1912.

GRANT MUSEUM OF ZOOLOGY

A much smaller collection in another part of London offers an overview of the animal kingdom that is brief but still somehow complete, making it one of the most fascinating museums in the city. The Grant Museum of Zoology in University Street houses the collection of University College London and is open to the public on weekday and Saturday afternoons. Here, crammed into a single galleried room, can be seen all manner of creatures in various forms, from preserved specimens of smaller animals, particularly fish, to a Micrarium: an alcove gallery of some 20,000 backlit microscope slides featuring a tiny proportion of the huge numbers of very small animals that make up 95 per cent of all animal life. Above all, there are bones wherever you look: the skeleton of a Siberian tiger, the skull of an African elephant, the skeletons of gorillas, orang-utans and chimpanzees, the shell of a Galapagos tortoise or the skeletons of two species of mammal thought to be extinct. These are the quagga, a subspecies of zebra wiped out by settlers to South Africa in the late nineteenth century, and the thylacine or Tasmanian tiger, thought to be extinct but possibly still alive on mainland Australia according to sightings reported in recent years.

SCIENCE MUSEUM

Next door to the Natural History Museum on Exhibition Road is the Science Museum. Founded in 1857 from the collection of the Royal Society of Arts, as well as objects collected from the Great Exhibition of 1851, it was originally part of the same institution that is now the Victoria and Albert Museum across the road, but became a dedicated science museum in 1909, taking up its current home a decade later. Since then, the museum collection has continued to expand to keep up with the massive advances in science – indeed, the definition of what we think of as science.

So there are nineteenth-century classics such as the oldest surviving James Watt steam engine, Stephenson's Rocket – the famous locomotive that won the competition to pull the world's first passenger service – or a working example of Charles Babbage's Difference Engine, arguably the world's first computer, built to Babbage's designs some 150 years after he drew them up. But there are also classics of the Space Age such as a Sputnik satellite or the command module from Apollo 10, the penultimate mission before the one that landed on the Moon. Today's museum is interactive and issue-based, engaging visitors in topics such as climate change, the information revolution, engineering as a way of shaping the future, and how the science of neurochemistry and genetics is changing the way we understand who we think we are.

MUSEUM OF LONDON

Anyone wanting to know about the history of this city needs to start at the Museum of London. Currently housed in a circular bunker of a building beside an excavated section of the original London Wall, it is due to move to new premises nearby – historic glass-roofed buildings that once formed part of Smithfield Market. The permanent collection is in part the fruit of earth turned over in the constant round of new building that has occurred all over London in recent decades, excavations that the museum's archaeologists have diligently monitored for artefacts and human remains. The museum collection tells a story of unbroken settlement since pre-Roman times; indeed, London had one great strategic advantage – a river navigable far upstream by ocean-going ships – which has made it Britain's principal city ever since.

Here we discover that a wooden Roman bridge pier, dated AD 85–90, was found at Pudding Lane, showing that the current site of London Bridge goes back some 2,000 years. But this was not the first bridge in London, as remnants of an even earlier structure, perhaps as old as BC 1700, were discovered at Vauxhall. Four metres across, it may have led to a now non-existent island in the centre of a river that was both wider and shallower in ancient times.

From these beginnings the museum takes the visitor on a journey across two millennia of political, commercial and social change, told through a great variety of objects and exhibits, from a reconstructed nineteenth-century wooden-walled debtors' cell that still bears the graffiti of its former occupants to an original Selfridges lift from the 1920s, like a time machine inviting you to step in and be whisked back to the age of the flappers and the Wall Street Crash. Just as spectacular is the Cauldron that London-based designer Thomas Heatherwick created for the Olympic flame and opening ceremony of the 2012 Games, which left such a vivid image of the city in the eyes of the world.

MUSEUM OF LONDON DOCKLANDS

The Museum of London Docklands can be found in No.1 Warehouse, West India Quay, in the shadow of Canary Wharf. More specific than its big sister, the Museum of London, it spells out the reason for London's success over the past 500 years through the stories of maritime trade that departed and returned to the city. For instance, there were not one but two separate whaling booms in which London was the pre-eminent port of call; indeed, by 1821 the 149 whaling ships operating out of the capital comprised the world's biggest fleet.

The museum takes the visitor along the river as the tide of commerce moved from wharves and warehouses in the Pool of London to new docks further east and eventually to those at Tilbury, closer to the sea, built to accommodate the huge container ships of today. But the most important story of all – the main reason for London's rise during the eighteenth century to its position as the leading global port – is the story of slavery and the sugar trade, to which the museum dedicates a large amount of space. Here we learn that William Beckford, Lord Mayor of London from 1762 until 1769, was also the richest plantation owner of the time, with more than 22 such establishments in the West Indies. Upon his death in 1770 Beckford's son, also called William, inherited an estate that today would be worth £110 million. Nearly two centuries later, in June 1948, the descendants of slaves arrived at Tilbury on the SS *Empire Windrush* to find work in a city that badly needed to replenish a labour force depleted by war.

NATIONAL MARITIME MUSEUM

Despite Britain's long history as a naval power and London's dominant position throughout the nineteenth century as the leading global port, the National Maritime Museum in Greenwich was created as recently as 1934. In addition to one of the most important collections of maritime art in the world, the museum also has extensive collections of artefacts relating to British maritime history, including William Kent's splendid royal barge – known as Prince Frederick's Barge – the uniform worn by Lord Nelson when he received his mortal wound at the Battle of Trafalgar in 1805 and a medal that was struck to mark the abolition of the slave trade.

The museum is now also the permanent home to *Nelson's Ship in a Bottle* (2010), one of the most successful works of contemporary art to have graced the fourth plinth in Trafalgar Square, beside **Nelson's Column**, since the series of public art commissions began there in 1999. Taking a scale model of HMS *Victory*, Nelson's flagship at Trafalgar, Anglo-Nigerian artist Yinka Shonibare dressed it with sails made of colourful African fabrics and placed the ship in a very large bottle, echoing a popular form of British folk art.

ROYAL OBSERVATORY

Royal Museums Greenwich, of which the National Maritime Museum is a part, also includes the Queen's House and, on top of a hill in nearby Greenwich Park, the Royal Observatory. This was founded in 1675 by King Charles II with the aim of finding the much sought-after reliable measurement of longitude – a task eventually mastered by clockmaker John Harrison's marine chronometer a century later, whose accuracy transformed navigation from then on. It is here at Greenwich that in 1884 the world's prime meridian was set by an international conference, and the Meridian Line is clearly marked for visitors as they stand and take in the spectacular view of Canary Wharf. Though the telescopes housed at the observatory are no longer in use, there is a popular planetarium on a site where the stars were once used to understand our place at sea and on land, as seen in the museum of astronomical and navigational tools now housed in the Observatory buildings.

RAF MUSEUM HENDON

London has a long maritime history but it was also one of the first places in Europe to see powered flight. Indeed, the Royal Air Force is the oldest national air force in the world, and one of its former airbases – RAF Hendon in Colindale, north London – which was a functioning aerodrome from 1908 until 1968, has been home to a superb collection of military aircraft since 1972. RAF Museum Hendon now has four huge hangars containing everything from a Blériot XI monoplane, the first aircraft to cross the English Channel, to a Harrier jump jet, and from a Wessex helicopter to a Short Sunderland flying boat. The most recently redeveloped hangar is the Grahame-White Factory building, which contains the largest collection of World War One aircraft anywhere in the world.

IMPERIAL WAR MUSEUM

As much as these flying machines are thrilling to see, most of them were designed to kill, and at the Imperial War Museum in Lambeth, south London (in a building that previously housed the Bethlem Royal Hospital, the mental hospital famous as 'Bedlam'), the predominant theme is the destructiveness of war. The museum's galleries cover most of the major modern conflicts in which Britain has been involved, from the highly acclaimed World War One galleries to the space devoted to recent conflicts in Iraq and Afghanistan, which confronts us with problems the world is still dealing with today. Throughout, incredibly affecting works of art reveal the human realities behind the information and objects on show, such as Colin Self's *Nuclear Victim (Beach Girl)* (1966), a disfigured sunbathing mannequin covered in cinders and black paint, or Jeremy Deller's *Baghdad, 5 March 2007* (2010), a 'ready-made' wreck of a real Baghdad car destroyed by a roadside bomb. Above all, there is the sobering Holocaust Exhibition, arranged over two floors: Britain's most significant memorial to a horror that must never be forgotten lest it should ever happen again.

WELLCOME COLLECTION

The Wellcome Collection on Euston Road is the best known of London's large group of museums devoted to the history, practice and applications of medicine. Since it first opened to the public in 2007, the Wellcome has become an essential haunt for those interested in the connections among art, culture, medical science, and attitudes to illness and death. Its permanent collection of medical artefacts is based on the extensive collection of Sir Henry Wellcome, founder of the Wellcome Trust, one of the world's largest medical charities. But the Wellcome also presents a diverse and highly original programme of temporary exhibitions, such as one exploring the modern study of sex in the West and another examining Tibetan Buddhist meditation and its effect on the mind.

SIR JOHN SOANE'S MUSEUM

Sir John Soane's Museum in Lincoln's Inn Fields may well be London's most eccentric museum. Soane was an architect, and in later life professor of architecture at the Royal Academy, whose career spanned the last five decades of the Georgian period. As a young man he embarked on a Grand Tour of Italy which marked him for life. His most famous surviving building is probably Dulwich Picture Gallery in southeast London, and his successful architectural practice furnished him with the resources to expand and develop his own house, now regarded as his greatest work. Beginning with a single terraced townhouse which he bought in 1792, over the next 30 years he bought two adjacent houses, and extensively and continuously remodelled them all in an architectural experiment whose results are still astounding today. The Soane Museum Act of 1833 was passed by Parliament to ensure that no. 13, the central house, and all its contents would be left to the nation; this was done in part to disinherit Soane's one surviving son, George, whose depravity had led him to write a defamatory article about his father published in the national press.

George's loss was the world's gain, as the house alone is nothing short of miraculous: like passing down a rabbit hole into a warren of unexpected spaces, with those at the rear, in particular, top-lit through coloured-glass roof lanterns that shed a mysterious light on the exotic contents beneath. These bountiful fruits of Soane's eclectic connoisseurship and lifelong collecting habit include: the alabaster sarcophagus of the Egyptian pharaoh

Seti I, bronzes from Pompeii, Greek vases, Chinese ceramics, Peruvian pottery and, in the picture gallery, the eight canvases of *A Rake's Progress* (1732–33) by William Hogarth. But it can also be said of this museum more than most that the whole is greater than the sum of its remarkable parts. In a way that is similar to 575 Wandsworth Road, architecture and art through some mysterious alchemy combine to create an environment both eccentric and sublime, which the *Oxford Dictionary of Architecture* describes as 'one of the most complex, intricate and ingenious series of interiors ever conceived'.

GEORGIAN LONDON

For most of the eighteenth century London was a peaceful city; but, whether you were rich or poor, it was certainly not safe. As Britain, and especially its capital, prospered from the developing Industrial Revolution and burgeoning international trade – alas, especially the slave trade – during the first half of the century, some 10,000 people were migrating to London every year. With population growth came the inevitable building boom, which included the first of the great garden squares, such as Grosvenor Square and Berkeley Square, still so characteristic of the city. But there was also poverty, squalor, chronic diseases, such as syphilis and smallpox, and crime. Notorious thieves such as Jack Sheppard, and the highwayman Dick Turpin and his Essex Gang are now romantic figures of folklore, though in reality they were thugs. These hazards aside, the rich and those who belonged to the prosperous middle class were thriving, but for the poor the situation could frequently be desperate. The drug of the day was gin, much cheaper than imported spirits and freely available. The result was an epidemic of alcoholism in London known as the Gin Craze, which was finally brought under control by the Gin Act of 1751. In the same year, the brutishness of life in the streets of Georgian London was memorably captured by William Hogarth in the print *Gin Lane*.

While the drinking habits of one class were a symptom of despair, the drinking craze of another was a marker of its increasing prosperity. The first coffee houses in Britain appeared in Oxford in the mid-seventeenth century and the fashion quickly spread to London. By the turn of the next century, there were some 2,000 such places where men of the middle and upper classes – women were not to be seen in these establishments – could go to drink coffee and discuss the issues of the day in polite, rational debates often with complete strangers. The first newspapers were then being produced in offices along Fleet Street, and coffee houses were places where you could go to read them and then talk about politics, science, the arts or other weighty matters (though not religion, which was off-limits) with your neighbour. As described by the leading man of letters in mid-Georgian London – Samuel Johnson, in *The Life of Dr Johnson*, the biography by his friend James Boswell – coffee houses were 'the constant Rendezvous for Men of Business, as well as the idle People, so that a Man is sooner ask'd about his Coffee-House than his Lodgings'. In fact, Dr Johnson – poet, critic and the man who compiled the first English dictionary – is known to have preferred tea, a beverage that would soon overtake coffee as both the capital's and the nation's favourite. But he relished the intellectual stimulation of the coffee house and could often be found taking supper with Boswell in the Turk's Head Coffee House in St Michael's

Alley, in the City. Meanwhile, Lloyd's Coffee House just around the corner in Lombard Street was popular with ship owners, merchants and ships' captains, and the tendency of the clientele to engage in shipping business led to the establishment of Lloyd's of London, the first and still the world's leading marine insurer.

Towards the end of the century, the popularity of coffee houses began to decline, and by then, too, crime in the city was being brought under control, in part because the first police force, known as the Bow Street Runners, was found to be an effective means of bringing offenders to justice. The force was set up in 1749 by Henry Fielding, a magistrate at the Bow Street court, who was also, as a novelist, one of the great chroniclers of eighteenth-century London life. The Runners were few in number but set a template for the more substantial state-funded force that would succeed them in the following century. However, there was one infamous outbreak of violence in London which they struggled to contain...

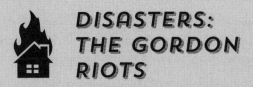

DISASTERS: THE GORDON RIOTS

Calamities can sometimes be self-inflicted. By the late eighteenth century, England, and then Britain, had been a Protestant country almost without interruption for some 250 years. Anti-Catholic laws, such as the Popery Act (1698), had reinforced the prohibitions on freedom of worship and involvement in public life which Catholics were forced to endure. In 1778, Britain was committed to a costly war in North America and needed to curry favour with British Catholics in an attempt to recruit more of them to the army, so the government passed the Papists Act, which allowed Catholics who renounced certain aspects of their faith some of the freedoms which had earlier been denied them. The new Act could hardly be described as liberal but went way too far for the President of the Protestant Association, Lord George Gordon. On 29 May 1780 he led a protest march on Parliament with some 50,000 people holding banners declaring 'No Popery' and demanding that the House of Commons repeal the Act. As is often the case when populist politicians whip up base prejudice, the protest soon flared into a riot, with members of the House of Lords being set upon as they left their carriages and tried to enter Parliament. Soon the fracas had metastasized into rioting across London, with Catholics rich and poor, along with their property, targeted in some of the attacks. The Bow Street Runners made a number of arrests but did not have the numbers to bring the violence under control. Finally, on 7 June, the army was called in. Around 285 rioters were shot dead and a further 200 wounded. More than 450 people were arrested, of whom a couple of dozen were later put to death.

ALONG THE RIVER: BATTERSEA POWER STATION TO WESTMINSTER BRIDGE

From Battersea the next bridge we pass under is Vauxhall Bridge, with the SIS (or MI6) Building on the South Bank, designed by Terry Farrell, looking like a Postmodern battleship – a decidedly conspicuous structure for what is the UK's secret intelligence service. A little further along, we get to Lambeth Bridge and Lambeth Palace to the south (in fact, at this point in the river's meander it's the west), the official residence of the Archbishop of Canterbury. From his study window, the archbishop must have a marvellous view downriver to one of London's greatest icons: the Palace of Westminster, the mother of all parliaments.

The name of that palace of democracy derives from an eighth-century Anglo-Saxon church, known as the West Minster, which at one time stood on the site, but the first palace there was built by the Danish King Cnut in the early eleventh century. When Cnut's palace later burnt down, Edward the Confessor built his own palace on the same spot, and this became the main residence for the kings of England until it also burnt down in 1512, at the start of the reign of Henry VIII. Westminster Hall, with its impressive hammerbeam ceiling, is the most substantial surviving part of the Old Palace, as the original building is referred to today.

Another palace was later built to accommodate Parliament, but this, too, burnt down in 1834, an event memorably captured on canvas by J. M. W. Turner in *The Burning of the Houses of Lords and Commons, October 16th, 1834* (1835). The New Palace, the magnificent Gothic Revival structure that today is so emblematic of London, was designed by Charles Barry and built over a period of 30 years, from 1840 to 1870, with decorations and architectural detailing in the Gothic style provided by Augustus Pugin. However, it is not an easy building either to update (its various services are antiquated and in some cases dangerous) or maintain (its stone fabric is crumbling away). At some point over the next few years, it seems likely that members of the Commons and the Lords will have to move out to another building while much needed renovations take place.

The Palace is another of London's UNESCO World Heritage Sites, along with the Abbey across the road and, of course, Elizabeth Tower: the name given to the neo-Gothic clock tower since the Queen's Diamond Jubilee Year in 2012. Completed in 1859, the tower is popularly but erroneously known as Big Ben, which is in fact the name of the huge bell that marks the hour after the famous Westminster Chimes.

PAINTING LONDON

Along with Paris and New York, London has a fair claim to the largest and most diverse range of art collections and exhibitions in the world. In fact, although Britain's first purpose-built national art galleries, Dulwich Picture Gallery and then the National Gallery, did not open until the early nineteenth century – later than counterparts in St Petersburg, Munich and Paris – the first public picture gallery was opened in 1746 at the Foundling Hospital in Coram's Fields, in Bloomsbury. Now the **Foundling Museum**, the collection, which includes works by William Hogarth, one of the hospital's main supporters, can still be seen there today. In the summer of 1769, the Royal Academy, founded the previous year, held its first exhibition, an annual event that has continued almost uninterrupted ever since. And gradually, over many decades through the nineteenth and twentieth centuries, private collections from the houses of wealthy Londoners have been bequeathed to major galleries or have opened in their own right. The latter include the Duke of Wellington's collection at **Apsley House** on Hyde Park Corner (the Neoclassical townhouse designed by Robert Adam with the rather grand address of Number One, London), with Francisco Goya's portrait of the Duke and tremendous works by Diego Velázquez. Another is the excellent collection at the refurbished **Kenwood House** in Hampstead, north London, with Rembrandt's mysterious *Self-Portrait with Two Circles* (1665), as well as the world-class holdings of the Wallace Collection and the Courtauld Gallery.

These alone would make London one of the world's great art capitals. But in the 1990s art experienced what amounted to a punk moment when a group of young British artists from Goldsmiths College in southeast London – the YBAs, as they are now known – began to show provocative and often deliberately offensive works that shook up the art world in the United Kingdom and sent shockwaves around the world. The movement announced itself in 1988 with a do-it-yourself show called 'Freeze' in a disused Docklands warehouse organised by the YBAs' prime mover and poster boy, Damien Hirst. Three further shows in similar spaces over the next couple of years cemented the group's output and attitude in the minds of London's art cognoscenti and, most tellingly, in that of one very important collector. The subsequent phenomenal popularity of Tate Modern in the shell of a former power station grew directly out of this anti-establishment aesthetic – though in fact Tate Modern is about as establishment as modern galleries come. But the contemporary London art scene – whose many private galleries, such as the **White Cube** galleries in Bermondsey and St James's or **Victoria Miro** in Shoreditch, can be every bit as stimulating – reflects the city itself in allowing the idiosyncratic, the anarchic, the confrontational, the marginal to shape the cultural norm. It's why so many artists from all over the world come to study there, and why so many art lovers follow them to absorb the edgy brilliance and richness of art in London.

NATIONAL GALLERY

The second most visited museum in the United Kingdom after the British Museum and one of the most visited art museums in the world, the National Gallery's collection is much smaller than those of major art museums such as the Louvre in Paris and the Metropolitan Museum in New York. Still, founded in 1824, it contains often superb paintings by more or less every major artist working before 1900.

The gallery's current Neoclassical home in Trafalgar Square was designed by William Wilkins and completed in 1838. But the collection continued to expand, so in 1991 the connecting Sainsbury Wing was added. Designed by Robert Venturi and Denise Scott Brown, and subsequently given over to Renaissance and pre-Renaissance art, this extension includes an exhibition space in the basement which in recent years has held groundbreaking displays of the works of Leonardo da Vinci and the late paintings of Rembrandt van Rijn.

The collection itself has so many highlights that to name a few risks distorting ideas of the overall quality of its holdings, but in areas such as 'golden age' British painting it is superlative, with national favourites such as J. M. W. Turner's *The Fighting Temeraire* (1839) or John Constable's *The Hay Wain* (1821), as well as classic works by George Stubbs, Thomas Gainsborough and Joseph Wright of Derby, demonstrating the brilliance of British painting in the Georgian era. The holdings also include superb paintings by some of the great European masters: Jan van Eyck's *The Arnolfini Portrait* (1434), Piero della Francesca's *The Baptism of Christ* (1448–50), Giovanni Bellini's *Portrait of Doge Leonardo Loredan* (1501), Leonardo's *The Virgin of the Rocks* (1483–86), Hans Holbein the Younger's *The Ambassadors* (1533), Caravaggio's *Supper at Emmaus* (1601), Peter Paul Rubens's *View of Het Steen in the Early Morning* (1636) and Georges Seurat's *Bathers at Asnières* (1884).

THE WALLACE COLLECTION

The Wallace Collection was bequeathed to the nation in its entirety in 1897 by the widow of the illegitimate son of the 4th Marquess of Hertford. Three years later it opened to the public in what is still its current home, Hertford House in Manchester Square, central London. In addition to significant holdings of European sculpture, arms and armour, the museum has internationally renowned collections of eighteenth-century ceramics, especially Sèvres porcelain, and French furniture from the same period. But, above all, its collection of Old Master paintings ranks among the finest in the world for a gallery of this size. As well as masterpieces such as *The Laughing Cavalier*

(1624) by Frans Hals, *Landscape with a Rainbow* (*c*.1638) by Rubens and Rembrandt's portrait of *The Artist's Son, Titus* (*c*.1657), the Wallace holds one of the finest collections of eighteenth-century French painting anywhere outside France, and certainly the finest in the UK. In addition to famous works such as *The Swing* (1757) by Jean-Honoré Fragonard and the portrait of *Madame de Pompadour* (1759) by François Boucher – one of many Bouchers it holds – the collection also has substantial numbers of paintings by Jean-Antoine Watteau and Jean-Baptiste Greuze.

THE COURTAULD GALLERY

The Courtauld Gallery is part of the Courtauld Institute of Art, founded by the industrialist Samuel Courtauld in 1932 and now one of the world's leading centres of art-historical research. Located in the part of Somerset House that faces the Strand in central London, the gallery contains a fine collection of Old Master paintings, including Lucas Cranach the Elder's famous *Adam and Eve* (1526), Pieter Bruegel the Elder's *Landscape with the Flight into Egypt* (1563) and a large number of superb smaller paintings by Rubens. But its core collection is made up of Impressionist and Post-Impressionist paintings – in particular, the largest group of works by Paul Cézanne in any UK museum. Highlights include Cézanne's *The Card Players* (1892–95), one of several versions he painted of this subject, Pierre-Auguste Renoir's *La Loge* (1874), Vincent Van Gogh's *Peach Blossoms in the Crau* (1889) and *Self-Portrait with Bandaged Ear* (1889), and *A Bar at the Folies-Bergère* (1882) by Édouard Manet, one of the great ambiguous masterpieces of Impressionism.

ROYAL ACADEMY OF ARTS

The Royal Academy of Arts was founded by a group of artists and architects in 1768 to promote the arts through a school dedicated to training artists and a programme of exhibitions disseminating knowledge and enjoyment of the arts to the public. Still run by a similar group of practitioner RAs, as members of the Academy are known, the institution is remarkable for having pursued that dual mission consistently for the two and a half centuries since then.

In 1867, the Academy moved into its current home at Burlington House in Piccadilly, a Neoclassical building originally designed by Lord Burlington in the eighteenth century. In fact, considering the size of the building, it is surprising that the Royal Academy's own collection is not on display, though it is possible to see a star piece, Michelangelo's sculpture of *The Virgin and Child with the Infant St John* (*c*.1504–05), known as the 'Taddei Tondo', outside the Sackler Galleries on the upper floor. Instead, in its two sets of galleries – the Sackler Wing opened in 1991 – the RA stages a year-round programme of internationally significant exhibitions, such as in 2015 a solo exhibition devoted to contemporary Chinese artist Ai Weiwei; and in 2016 shows focusing on early modern painting inspired by gardens, the art of Giorgione and his sixteenth-century Venetian contemporaries, and the range and influence of Abstract Expressionist painting.

In other words, its programme is broader in historical scope than that of any other gallery in London. Indeed, throughout the 1980s and 1990s, before the opening of Tate Modern in 2000 stole a lot of its modern and contemporary thunder, the daring blockbuster shows put on here by former head of exhibitions Sir Norman Rosenthal tended to make the curatorial weather in London. This ability to grab the headlines was encapsulated in the show Sensation, the groundbreaking, taboo-busting 1997 exhibition of work by the then increasingly confrontational YBAs, which featured pieces by the likes of Damien Hirst, and especially Jake and Dinos Chapman, which are still shocking today.

But the RA is also an art school and as an institution, it remains committed to the work of living artists, in particular through its Summer Exhibition, to which any member of the public can submit work. This show has been held in the main galleries almost every summer since 1769 and still features a huge number of works, all selected by a committee of Academy members.

TATE MODERN

Tate Modern is the most visited modern art museum in the world. Since opening in 2000, it has changed perceptions of modern and contemporary art among the general public in

Britain, and especially among the young. Suddenly, thanks to this brilliantly redeveloped post-industrial building on the south bank of the Thames, as well as the in-your-face attitude of the YBAs, whose work was reaching peak exposure at the time it opened, contemporary art in the new millennium was cool.

The former Bankside Power Station had been in danger of demolition until, in 1994, the Tate took possession of it and appointed the architects Herzog and de Meuron to convert it into a temple of modern art. The result was hailed as a game-changer for art museums, with the massive Turbine Hall, Tate Modern's giant atrium, overwhelming the visitor with a cathedral-like hush and awe. This cavernous space is the site of a prestigious commission given every year to a distinguished international artist to fulfil. Most of those who have done it have described it as a daunting challenge, but that hasn't stopped a roll-call of some of the biggest names in contemporary art from taking it on – among them Louise Bourgeois, whose giant spider was the first such commission; Olafur Eliasson, whose huge yellow sun was like a religious experience for many who saw it; and Carsten Höller, whose giant slides were more funfair than fine art.

In addition to the three floors of galleries devoted to the Tate's collection of international modern art, one of the finest and most comprehensive in the world, the museum also stages significant temporary exhibitions. In 2015 and 2016, this programme featured the work of a succession of twentieth- and twenty-first-century female artists, addressing the traditional masculine bias in ideas about art history.

In the past few years, the already gargantuan building has been further extended, with subterranean spaces for performance art, known as the Tanks, opened up in three converted oil tanks in 2012. Then 2016 saw the opening of a ten-storey extension, the Switch House, a misshapen ziggurat developed from the old adjoining switch house, with four floors of galleries devoted to contemporary conceptual art.

TATE BRITAIN

These days Tate Britain rather plays second fiddle to its standout sibling a few minutes downriver by high-speed ferry. But the gallery still holds the finest collection of British art in the UK. Based at Millbank, on the north bank of the Thames close to Vauxhall Bridge, the Tate is based in yet another of London's many Neoclassical temples of culture, founded by Sir Henry Tate, the famous sugar magnate. Since Tate Modern now houses the international modern art, Tate Britain has more space to display the collection of British art from 1500 to the present. As well as staging regular temporary exhibitions, it also plays host most years to the once-controversial Turner Prize, showing work by each of the four contenders shortlisted for the award each year.

Tate Britain is also custodian to the Turner Bequest: the contents of the studio of J. M. W. Turner – paintings, prints and drawings – which the artist himself left to the nation, the largest collection of his work anywhere in the world. It is accessed by a separate outside entrance to a Postmodern annex known as the Clore Gallery, designed by Sir James Stirling, which opened in 1987.

NATIONAL PORTRAIT GALLERY

When it opened in 1856, the National Portrait Gallery was the first gallery in the world devoted solely to that genre. Since 1897, it has occupied a building just around the corner from the National Gallery, where it welcomes more than a million visitors every year. The collection of portraits of famous figures from British history comprises paintings, drawings, miniatures and photographs, including the famous Chandos portrait of William Shakespeare, Robert Howlett's memorable photograph of Isambard Kingdom Brunel, and Paula Rego's wonderfully informal portrait of the writer and academic Germaine Greer. Recent temporary exhibitions have included a show on Picasso's approach to portraiture; a series of portraits of ordinary people using different mediums by the contemporary artist Grayson Perry, exploring modern notions of identity; and a posthumous retrospective of the paintings of Lucian Freud, one of the great British painters of the late twentieth century.

DULWICH PICTURE GALLERY

Designed by Sir John Soane and opened in 1817, Dulwich Picture Gallery, at Dulwich in southeast London, was the UK's first purpose-built public art gallery. In its use of illumination through overhead skylights, a strategy Soane had already trialled in his house at Lincoln's Inn, Dulwich exerted a big influence on the way art galleries ever since have been designed. Its permanent collection is still among the finest holdings of Old Master paintings in Britain, including Rembrandt's much-loved *Girl at a Window* (1645), as well as important paintings by Peter Paul Rubens, Nicolas Poussin and Bartolomé Esteban Murillo. The programme of temporary exhibitions stands out from other London galleries in often choosing to explore classic work that falls outside the established canon of European and American art. Shows in recent years have exposed patrons to the work of neglected British modernist Winifred Knights, early twentieth-century Norwegian landscape painter Nikolai Astrup and the Canadian modernist Emily Carr.

SAATCHI GALLERY

The huge global success of contemporary British art would almost certainly not have happened without Charles Saatchi. The former advertising magnate was quick to recognise the impact of the new art being created by the YBAs and bought extensively from the likes of Hirst, the Chapman Brothers and Sarah Lucas as a result of their early warehouse shows. Saatchi already owned a gallery in St John's Wood, north London, just off Abbey Road where, in a 1987 exhibition that heavily influenced the YBAs, he was the first curator in Britain to show the work of future global art star Jeff Koons.

The Sensation show at the Royal Academy drew exclusively from what by 1997 was Saatchi's huge collection of works by the YBAs. By this time, his unquenchable curiosity had led him to purchase work by other, younger artists, and in 2008 the Saatchi Gallery opened at new premises at the redeveloped Chelsea Barracks on the King's Road. It is now London's most visited private gallery, showing work by a truly global roster of contemporary artists.

THE VICTORIA AND ALBERT MUSEUM

The Victoria and Albert Museum is the largest museum of decorative art and design in the world. It came into being following the Great Exhibition of 1851 and for many years was known as the South Kensington Museum, only changing its name officially to the current one some 50 years later, towards the end of Queen Victoria's reign. For a long time, it held a joint remit as a museum of science and the arts, but in 1909 the two collections separated since when the V&A has dedicated itself to the fine and decorative arts.

The V&A has a collection of over 4.5 million objects, so it is physically impossible to show more than a fraction at any one time. Despite this, taking in the breadth of what is displayed is a significant undertaking for any visitor, as the collection represents more than 2,000 years of the aesthetic traditions of many cultures, especially those of Europe and Asia.

The Asian holdings, which occupy several galleries, encompass the traditions of Korean, Chinese and Japanese arts, including wonderful kimonos and impressive suits of Samurai armour. The centrepiece of the Jameel Gallery of Islamic Art is the world-famous Ardabil Carpet, but everywhere in this room exquisite ceramics and intricately patterned tiles offer reminders of the great cultural achievements of the Islamic world. In another dedicated gallery are examples of the extensive South and South-East Asian collections, the most important in the West with more than 6,000 paintings and over 60,000 items in total. These objects include 'Tipu's Tiger', the famous wooden automaton made in the late eighteenth century for Tipu Sultan, the ruler of Mysore.

In European art, the V&A houses stupendous treasures, with a superb collection of Italian sculpture including pieces by Donatello, Rossellino and Canova, and especially Gian Lorenzo Bernini's magnificent *Neptune and Triton* (1622–23). This can be found in the recently refurbished Baroque galleries (1600–1815), which feature extraordinary objects – armoires, dresses, clocks, ceremonial jugs, tulip holders – and even entire rooms transplanted to a museum where, given the strange context, they exert a fascination as disconcerting as an installation of contemporary art. One such example is the Music Room from the now-demolished Norfolk House in St James's Square, London. There are whole sections of the museum dedicated to pre-Renaissance art going back to the Roman period, as well as to metalwork, glass or various other mediums of decorative art. And in painting, the V&A has world-renowned exhibits, such as the gigantic Raphael Cartoons: the paintings that Raphael made to be turned into tapestries for the walls of the Sistine Chapel in Rome. The museum also has one of the largest collections in the world of work by John Constable, including many of his celebrated oil sketches.

But as if the bewildering variety and quality of the treasures wasn't enough, the V&A also stages an adventurous programme of temporary exhibitions which in recent years has featured the work of modern icons such as David Bowie and Alexander McQueen, both sell-out events; new spaces for temporary exhibitions open in 2017 to better accommodate the large crowds drawn by such blockbuster shows.

LATE GEORGIAN AND EARLY VICTORIAN LONDON

Queen Victoria was the last monarch from the House of Hanover, which ruled the United Kingdom for nearly two centuries, beginning with George I in 1714. By 1837, when Victoria ascended the throne, the fabric of modern London had more or less assumed its current form, with the elegant grandeur of John Nash's Regent Street and Oxford Circus – built during the Regency period and the decade that followed – among the major architectural achievements of the first half of the century. Following the completion of the first Westminster Bridge in 1750, other permanent Thames crossings were erected at regular intervals, and within the space of a few decades the two separate parts of the city – north and south of the river – were linked all along its length as far as London Bridge, itself rebuilt in 1831. A sense of the optimism that such improvements brought can be gleaned from the largest canvas John Constable ever painted, *The Opening of Waterloo Bridge, Whitehall Stairs, June 18th, 1817* (1832), which took him 13 years to finish and is now on display as part of the Turner Collection at Tate Britain's Clore Gallery.

While the roads and bridges undoubtedly made London more accessible, another revolution reshaped the city's relations not only with itself, but also with the rest of Britain. Beginning in 1836, the great railway terminuses whose hundreds of lines fan out to all parts of the country took root around the city centre: London Bridge in 1836, Euston in 1837, Paddington in 1838, Fenchurch Street in 1841, Waterloo in 1848 and King's Cross in 1850 were followed in the next few decades by Victoria (1860), Charing Cross (1864), Cannon Street (1866), St Pancras (1868), Liverpool Street (1874) and Marylebone (1898). With them came a new kind of civic architecture made of plate glass and cast iron, creating exalted spaces like the impressive train shed at Paddington, built by Isambard Kingdom Brunel for his Great Western Railway in 1854, which provoked comparisons with England's ancient cathedrals.

Sadly, the building which has most come to symbolise the optimism and adventure of the Early Victorian period, and whose engineering innovations were a template for some of the great railway terminuses, has been long since destroyed. The Crystal Palace, designed by Joseph Paxton, was the centrepiece of the Great Exhibition of 1851, a world's fair. It was the brainchild of the inventor Henry Cole and the Queen's husband, Prince Albert himself, and was intended to show the British people the many wonders of the manufacturing age which Britain's own Industrial Revolution had enabled, alongside technology and products from other nations and cultural spoils from countries then falling under the yoke of the British Empire. The Crystal Palace was built in Hyde Park at the end of Exhibition Road, on the site where the **Albert Memorial** now stands, and many of its exhibits went on to form parts of the collections of what today are the Victoria and Albert Museum and the Science Museum nearby, in the area known as Albertopolis. In 1854 the spectacular greenhouse was moved to what is now Crystal Palace Park in southeast London. There it remained for decades until in 1936 it burnt down, and with that one of the great events in the history of London passed somewhat into myth.

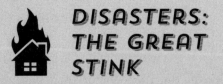

DISASTERS: THE GREAT STINK

Although a glass palace was meant to convince Londoners that theirs was the most modern of cities, in the 1850s they only had to open their windows to be reminded of its longstanding problems. Between 1801 and 1861 London's population tripled in size, from one to three million, so that the overcrowding, the squalor and the deprivation in the poorer areas was becoming an endemic misery and, as both foreigners and Londoners observed, a shameful contrast to the more prosperous central districts. At the most precarious level of existence, there was either the debtors' prison or, for the truly destitute, the workhouse: horrific environments laid bare by Charles Dickens – Victorian London's great narrative conscience – in the novels *Little Dorrit* (1857) and *Oliver Twist* (1838).

The growth in population also brought an increase in effluent that filled the many cesspools under London's streets to bursting point. In 1847 an edict was issued directing all human waste to be discharged into the city's sewers, so that the Thames itself became 'a Stygian pool reeking with ineffable and unbearable horror', as it was later described by future prime minister Benjamin Disraeli. Once it had been home to many types of fish – even salmon – and all manner of waterfowl, including the mute swan, the royal bird; all of these creatures rapidly disappeared. And human health was directly affected: in 1849 more than 14,000 people died in the worst outbreak of cholera ever to have hit the capital; then in 1854 a number in excess of 10,000 also perished.

Disraeli was well qualified to pass judgement, as Parliament, where he sat as an MP, was particularly disrupted by the river's malodour. In the hot summer of 1858, MPs resorted to hanging sheets soaked in chlorine over the windows of the Commons chamber to try to mask what was dubbed the Great Stink. Finally, with the problem on its own doorstep, Parliament was forced to act. The engineer Joseph Bazalgette was called upon, and the solution he found involved massive new outfall sewers to the north and south of the city, and more than 1,000 miles of new street sewers underground; it also saw the construction of the Victoria, Albert and Chelsea Embankments along the Thames in central London, which allowed new main roads and underground lines to be built on what had been fetid marshy land in the centre of the city. Bazalgette's comprehensive new system took until 1875 to complete and is considered one of the great engineering achievements of the Victorian period.

ALONG THE RIVER: WESTMINSTER BRIDGE TO THE MILLENNIUM BRIDGE

We have now reached a stretch of the Thames where famous sights greet us continuously from both banks of the river. On the South Bank, beyond County Hall – the old headquarters of the Greater London Council and now home to the London Aquarium – we see the London Eye, one of London's millennium year landmarks and a tourist favourite that was the world's tallest Ferris wheel at the time it was built. Beyond this are the two Golden Jubilee pedestrian bridges, completed in 2002, the fiftieth anniversary year of the reign of Queen Elizabeth II. Sandwiched between them is Hungerford Bridge, the rail viaduct spanning the river from Charing Cross Station on the north bank to Waterloo East station on the south.

As we pass beneath these crossings, we see the Southbank Centre, whose most prominent building is the Royal Festival Hall, while on the Victoria Embankment to the north, the Ancient Egyptian obelisk known as Cleopatra's Needle still stands where it was first erected in 1878. In fact, this monument has nothing to do with Cleopatra, dating from the reign of the pharaoh Hatshepsut some 3,500 years ago, but was brought to London from Alexandria, where Cleopatra held court a millennium and a half later.

Under Waterloo Bridge – not the structure depicted by Constable but a modern replacement completed in 1945 – we pass the National Theatre on the South Bank and Somerset House on the north, before going under the two Blackfriars Bridges – first the road bridge and then the recently renovated rail bridge whose 4,400 photovoltaic panels made it the world's largest solar-powered bridge when it reopened in 2014.

Up ahead are two of London's major landmarks on opposite sides of the river: St Paul's Cathedral in the City and Tate Modern at Bankside. These are now linked by the Millennium Bridge, a steel suspension bridge for pedestrians which was forced to close on its opening day in 2000 when the number of people using it caused it to wobble alarmingly. It was back to the drawing board for the architects, Foster and Partners, and their engineers, Arup Group, who introduced a series of fluid dampers that stabilised what is now a very popular crossing of the Thames.

ACTING LONDON

London is one of the world's great centres of the theatrical arts. If we allow that it might have been used for performances other than blood sports, we could trace the city's theatrical heritage back to the Roman amphitheatre discovered and now partially on display beneath the Guildhall Art Gallery. We also know that in the medieval period temporary theatres set up inside barns or galleried inns were a feature of the city's rambunctious social life, but the first permanent structures coincide with the flowering of English culture that occurred during the reign of Gloriana, Queen Elizabeth I, in the late sixteenth century.

The early theatres seem to have formalised the medieval model so that the great theatres of Shakespeare's day, as we can see from the rebuilt Globe Theatre now on its original site at Southwark, followed a similar circular design: stacked floors of galleries surrounding the stage and a standing area in front of it. In the following century, the masques at the court in Whitehall introduced the proscenium arch, conceived by Inigo Jones, which became a standard stage frame in subsequent theatre design.

Alas, during the Civil War and the subsequent Commonwealth, the Puritans who had taken control of London closed all the theatres and even demolished the Globe, considering the art form to be detrimental to public morality.

Mercifully, this proved a temporary setback, as Charles II was a theatre lover to his bones and also a lover of women, so he issued a decree that female roles should hitherto be played only by female actors. In the Restoration period, theatre once again flourished, especially the king's favoured genre of comedy, and new theatres such as the Theatre Royal, Drury Lane, received the monarch's explicit approval.

The following century saw developments good and bad in London theatre: the influence of actor–manager David Garrick, who introduced a new realism to his performances which remains the template for actors today; in 1728, the first production of the world's first musical, *The Beggar's Opera* by John Gay; and in 1737, infamously, the passing of the Theatrical Licensing Act, which required all new plays to be vetted by the Lord Chamberlain for approval or prohibition. Exerting a deadening effect on the ambitions of London playwrights and theatre managers, the Act was not repealed until 1968. Nonetheless, Theatreland – as the gaggle of West End theatres is collectively known – continued to grow throughout the eighteenth and nineteenth centuries, and figures such as Richard Brinsley Sheridan and Oscar Wilde wrote stage works, premiered in London, which are still performed all over the English-speaking world.

In the nineteenth century came a new kind of variety theatre unique to Britain, known as the music hall. Originally staged in pubs, music hall shows – which featured singing, comedy and variety acts – catered to the rapidly expanding working class both in the prosperous West End but also in the areas where they lived. East End venues such as **Wilton's Music Hall** in Whitechapel, a beautiful 'giant pub hall' opened in 1859 and in recent years restored to something like its Victorian prime, runs a theatrical programme in keeping with those traditions, offering a glimpse of what was a thriving form of theatre until the 1950s – one that has also left us wonderful songs, such as 'The Boy I Love Is Up In the Gallery' (1885) by George Ware, or Leigh and Collins's 'My Old Man (Said Follow the Van)' (1919), which offer vivid snapshots of working-class London life.

As well as music halls, other professional houses emerged in quantity in the late nineteenth and early twentieth centuries in the West End and other parts of the city. There are now some 241 professional theatres in London, including around 135 houses subsidised by the Arts Council of Great Britain, such as the National Theatre on the South Bank. Moreover, a theatrical renaissance in the past century has seen first performances in London theatres of classic plays by a succession of brilliant British dramatists from Noël Coward to John Osborne, Harold Pinter, Tom Stoppard and Caryl Churchill – to name just a few of the very best. But London theatre in recent decades has also been home to long-running productions of popular musicals, such as Claude-Michel Schönberg's *Les Misérables* (West End, 1985) and Andrew Lloyd Webber's *The Phantom of the Opera* (1986), both of which have notched up over 12,000 unbroken performances and are still going strong. The quality and breadth of London's theatrical offerings are one of the main reasons why tourists from Britain and abroad flock to the capital in such large numbers every year.

NATIONAL THEATRE

The National Theatre is located beside the complex of arts venues known as the Southbank Centre, on the Thames. The National Theatre Company was formed in 1963 under the legendary British actor Sir Laurence Olivier, and for the next 13 years was based at the Old Vic near Waterloo before, in 1976, it moved to its current home: a Brutalist building designed by Sir Denys Lasdun, whose aesthetic qualities still divide opinion.

As a publicly funded theatre – in addition to adventurous productions of classic repertoire from Euripides through Shakespeare to Tennessee Williams – the National can afford to stage often challenging new work by contemporary playwrights, which has resulted in memorable productions of some of the finest British plays of the past 40 years in its three auditoria: the Olivier Theatre, its main venue, the smaller Lyttleton Theatre, and the studio theatre once called the Cottesloe Theatre and now known as the Dorfman Theatre. Among the best have been *Amadeus* (1979–80) by Peter Shaffer, *Pravda* by Howard Brenton and David Hare (1985), *The Madness of George III* (1991) by Alan Bennett, Tom Stoppard's *Arcadia* (1993), *Copenhagen* (1998) by Michael Frayn, *The History Boys* (2004) by Alan Bennett, *War Horse* (2007–09), based on the novel by

Michael Morpurgo, and *The Curious Incident of the Dog in the Night-Time* (2012), based on the novel by Mark Haddon. Many of these productions have subsequently transferred to the West End, where in some cases they have enjoyed extended runs, as have a good number of the productions of classic musicals in which the National seems to excel.

ROYAL SHAKESPEARE COMPANY AT THE BARBICAN

After a period of absence, the Royal Shakespeare Company, or RSC, is once again based for part of the year at the Barbican Theatre, the London home that was expressly designed for its needs. The theatre is one element of the Barbican Centre, the biggest arts centre in Europe, which in addition comprises a further small theatre, known as the Pit, along with two important art gallery spaces, a 2,000-seat concert hall that is home to the London Symphony Orchestra and a three-screen cinema complex, as well as restaurants, conference halls, trade exhibition spaces and even the second-biggest conservatory in London: a tropical roof garden in the heart of the City.

The Barbican Centre, which opened in 1982 on a site which had been heavily bombed in World War Two, is only one element of the vast Barbican Estate, named for the site of the old Roman fort on which it is built. Now regarded as a classic of Brutalist architecture, it was designed by the practice of Chamberlin, Powell and Bon, who had previously designed the neighbouring

Golden Lane Estate. The Barbican Estate was on an altogether different scale and, in addition to the Barbican Centre, includes the Museum of London, a music conservatoire, a library and a girls' school, as well as a large number of residential flats. Indeed, its most prominent landmarks are three residential towers which until recently were the tallest in the capital.

The RSC's productions of Shakespeare have been world-renowned since it was first established as a permanent company in 1959 by Sir Peter Hall, shortly before the emergence of the National Theatre. Officially based in Stratford-upon-Avon, the birthplace of the Bard, the company's Barbican season runs during the winter months. At other times of the year both the Barbican Theatre and the Pit host productions of theatre and also dance, featuring some of the most innovative companies from around the world.

GLOBE THEATRE

The opening of a new Globe Theatre in 1997, close to the site at Bankside where some four centuries earlier the original had stood, is due in large part to the energy and vision of one man, the American actor and director Sam Wanamaker. It was he who for more than 20 years after founding the Shakespeare Globe Trust in 1970 defied the naysayers to bring into being a new version of Shakespeare's famous theatre. The original was built in 1599 for the Lord Chamberlain's Men, the company for whom Shakespeare both wrote and acted, though this was replaced after it burnt down in 1613, the year (some say) the Bard wrote his final play. Allowing for compromises required by modern safety regulations, as well as the lack of documentation as to the exact design of the original, the new Globe attempts to recreate the kind of environment in which these plays were first performed. In that regard, the half-timbered building is in fact a composite of what is known of various Elizabethan theatres, as opposed to a replica of the original Globe.

Productions of Shakespeare's plays at the theatre have attempted as far as possible to recreate the original conditions of performance. In addition to the presence of standing spectators in front of the stage, known in Shakespeare's time as groundlings, the theatre, which like the original is open to the elements, stages plays only in the summer months and has resisted using spotlights or modern sound-projection systems. All music is performed live and one production of *Twelfth Night*, directed in 2002 by Mark Rylance – the Globe's first artistic director – used an all-male cast. Some would say this is taking authenticity too far. But the Globe, which now also has an indoor theatre – the Sam Wanamaker Playhouse, built in the slightly later Jacobean style – offers a fascinating glimpse into the golden age of Elizabethan theatre, one of Britain's and especially London's greatest gifts to the world.

THEATRE ROYAL, DRURY LANE

There has been a Theatre Royal, Drury Lane since the first one opened in 1663 with the official blessing of King Charles

II, making it now the oldest in London to have continuously occupied a single site. But the first theatre, which specialised in Restoration comedies by William Wycherley and John Dryden – the leading exponents of the genre – and was a pioneer in giving roles to female actors such as Nell Gwyn, was not a great commercial success. In 1672 that original building burned down and was replaced two years later by a new theatre which, over the next century, would be managed by illustrious figures such as David Garrick and Richard Brinsley Sheridan. In 1791, Sheridan took the drastic decision to demolish what by then was a very old-fashioned building but the replacement, which opened in 1794, while a practical improvement, proved to be an economic headache.

Fire remained a constant problem for theatres and, in this regard, the new Theatre Royal was truly state-of-the-art, pioneering safety features such as the now standard iron safety curtain separating auditorium and stage, and even including a water tank on the roof for emergency use in extinguishing fires. But the new building was also huge, accommodating some 3,600 people, making it more than 50 per cent larger than any West End theatre of today. The Theatre Royal was also one of only two original 'patent theatres' permitted by Charles II's Patent Act to stage serious spoken-word drama, i.e. plays without music – an act not revoked until 1833. But Sheridan's grand new theatre was utterly unsuited to the intimacy required for serious drama and the dramatist–manager resorted instead to putting on spectacular productions that would draw in the large crowds needed to cover the costs of the enormous house.

Then, despite all the improvements, in 1809 the theatre again burned down, an event that Sheridan, now facing ruin, viewed with sanguine resignation. The new building, the fourth and current Theatre Royal, was completed in 1812 and is regarded today as one of the most beautiful in London. In 1817, it became the first British theatre to be entirely gaslit, but mod cons were not enough on their own to draw in the punters. Its patent status was a commercial millstone and the theatre continued to struggle throughout the nineteenth century, with audiences increasingly turning away from serious theatre towards more popular entertainments. In the twentieth century, and especially since 1945, it seems to have abandoned its high calling altogether, devoting itself almost exclusively to musicals: the theatrical genre that for hundreds of years in one form or another has been the most popular with the public and which today keeps many West End theatres afloat. The Theatre Royal is now owned by Andrew Lloyd Webber's Really Useful Group, though it is yet to stage one of his own shows.

AN INCOMPLETE TOUR OF THEATRELAND FROM SHAFTESBURY AVENUE TO THE STRAND

Theatreland refers to a wide area of the West End in which some 40 central London theatres including the Theatre Royal, Drury Lane can be found. But there are certain streets, such as Haymarket and the Strand, that are particularly associated with West End theatre and probably the most famous of all is Shaftesbury Avenue. Regarded as the heart of Theatreland, the street contains four more or less adjacent theatres – the **Lyric, Apollo, Gielgud** and **Queen's Theatres** – along its northern side, as well as the **Palace Theatre** at Cambridge Circus, the junction with Charing Cross Road. Beginning here, if we start to walk south along Charing Cross Road, we pass first the **Wyndham's Theatre** and then the **Garrick Theatre.** Then turning left into St Martin's Lane, we pass the **Duke of York's Theatre** and the **Noël Coward Theatre,** which in 1960 – then known as the New Theatre – staged the first production of Lionel Bart's *Oliver!*, perhaps the greatest British musical of all and probably the best ever written about London.

Walking up St Martin's Lane, we pass the **Arts Theatre** in Great Newport Street, off to the left, and then a little further on we take a left turn into West Street and come to **St Martin's Theatre,** where Agatha Christie's *The Mousetrap* – the longest-running play in history – is still drawing in the crowds after more than 26,000 performances. Opening in 1952, the year the current monarch ascended the throne, it played first at the **Ambassadors Theatre** next door before transferring in 1974 to St Martin's, where it continues its indefinite run. Unlike the rest of Christie's work, the play has never been filmed, and the queen of detective fiction herself asked the audience not to reveal the surprise ending to anyone who hadn't yet seen it – an *omertà* that held up with astonishing persistence until Wikipedia spilled the beans in 2010. But still the punters come, suggesting that the vow of secrecy which held for so long was a piece of counterintuitive marketing genius with a mystique all of its own.

Retracing our steps, we continue north along Monmouth Street to Seven Dials and its esoteric sundials column, with the **Cambridge Theatre** on the corner of Mercer Street and Earlham Street, from where a little detour would bring us to the excellent **Donmar Warehouse**, which since its opening in 1977 has staged some of the most stimulating productions of both contemporary and classic plays anywhere in London. Returning to Seven Dials and walking further north along Monmouth Street, we reach the northern end of Shaftesbury Avenue and then High Holborn, passing the **Shaftesbury Theatre**, before turning into Drury Lane and passing the **New London Theatre**, where Lord Lloyd Webber's *Cats* ran for exactly 21 years over almost 9,000 performances – the record for a musical until this was overtaken by *Les Misérables*.

Carrying on down Drury Lane, we pass the rear of the Theatre Royal, whose entrance is in fact in Catherine Street, before reaching the **Aldwych Theatre**. Curving around Aldwych to the west, we pass the **Novello Theatre** and glimpse the **Duchess** and

Lyceum Theatres in side streets leading back to Covent Garden, before we hit the Strand. If we carry on down the north side of the Strand towards Charing Cross, we pass the **Vaudeville Theatre** before reaching the **Adelphi Theatre**, which has existed on this site in various incarnations since 1806, with the current name being adopted in 1819. Today's Adelphi was reopened in 1930 with a radical Art Deco design, but in that regard another even more famous theatre on the south side of the street had already shown the way the previous year.

THE SAVOY THEATRE

The Savoy Theatre has long been a constituent part of the building that includes the **Savoy Hotel,** with its magnificent Art Deco entrance accessed by Savoy Court, the very short road which remains the only street in Britain in which cars are obliged to drive on the right-hand side. The original theatre was built in 1881 for the D'Oyly Carte Opera Company, which staged the hugely popular comic operas of W. S. Gilbert and Arthur Sullivan. Richard D'Oyly Carte was an impresario, as well as a composer in his own right, and the handsome profits from the theatre were ploughed into the building of the world-famous hotel.

The Savoy Theatre, which saw the premieres of every Gilbert and Sullivan opera from *Patience* onwards, was the first public building in the world to be wholly lit by electricity. In the years following the death of Sullivan in 1900 and D'Oyly Carte in

1901, the ultramodern theatre staged a variety of musical productions, some with lyrics written by Gilbert in his career after Sullivan. Then in 1915, D'Oyly Carte's son Rupert took control of the venue, and it was under his wing that the Art Deco modernisation of 1929 took place. The theatre continued to stage productions of Gilbert and Sullivan throughout the 1930s and in 1941 saw the premiere of Noël Coward's *Blithe Spirit*. The theatre and hotel remained the family business until the 1980s, but then in 1990, in the middle of a renovation, a fire broke out that gutted the building. Against the odds, by piecing together the décor of 60 years earlier, the Savoy Theatre was superbly restored to its Art Deco splendour and today continues to stage, among other things, the repertoire for which it was originally built.

OLD VIC

We could easily continue our walking tour through Trafalgar Square and along Haymarket, where in addition to **Her Majesty's Theatre** we find the **Theatre Royal, Haymarket**: one of the oldest theatres in London, originally built in 1720 and redesigned by John Nash in the Neoclassical style a century later. But some of London's best theatre experiences are to be had in venues outside the centre and among the best of which is the Old Vic.

Located at one end of a road known as the Cut, behind Waterloo Station, the theatre now known as the Old Vic was established in 1818 as the Royal Cobourg Theatre, which in 1833 became the Royal Victoria Theatre. It was rebuilt in 1871 and renamed the Royal Victoria Palace, but it seems to have been known affectionately since that period as the Old Vic. In the twentieth century, it has earned a deserved reputation as one of the most serious playhouses in London. It was led during the late 1920s by John Gielgud, and during the 1950s attracted the likes of Ralph Richardson and Laurence Olivier to productions staged by the Old Vic Company. In 1963, under Olivier's leadership, this became the National Theatre Company, which remained at the venue until the opening of the National in 1976.

Since the 1980s, it has had several very distinguished artistic directors, including Jonathan Miller, Sir Peter Hall and, most surprisingly – from 2003 until 2014 – the American actor Kevin Spacey. The Hollywood star brought with him both cachet and class, turning in some brilliant performances in a programme of mostly classic repertoire, both as actor and director, and giving the Old Vic its highest profile since Olivier's day.

ROYAL COURT THEATRE

The Royal Court has been the most artistically adventurous theatre in London for more than half a century. Its current venue, in Sloane Square at the eastern end of the King's Road, opened in 1888, but the Royal Court's reputation as the leading theatre for new and often very controversial plays dates from the 1950s, when classics such as John Osborne's *Look Back in Anger* (1956) – the play which introduced the Angry Young Man to British cultural life – received their premieres there. Since then, the list of first productions by some of the finest writers in successive generations is impressive and includes works by Arnold Wesker, Howard Brenton, Caryl Churchill, Hanif Kureishi and Sarah Kane. In its commitment to new writing, the Royal Court is a vital organ in the continuing health of contemporary British theatre.

IMPERIAL CITY:
THE PROSPERITY...

By the late nineteenth century, London was the most modern city in the world, grown rich on the profits of Britain's vast and expanding empire – the largest the world has ever seen. Electric streetlamps were introduced to the capital in 1878, the same year they arrived in Paris, its main rival at the time. But one invention, which would revolutionise transport not only in London but, over the next century, in cities around the world, was so daring in its ambition that people considered it a hellish proposition, though very soon tens of thousands of passengers came to see it as an indispensable public good.

By the 1860s, London's population was so large and the traffic so dense that getting across the city by road took even longer than it does today. So a radical solution was suggested: an underground railway – the first in the world – built by cutting a deep ditch and covering it over. The new line, which opened in 1863, was known as the Metropolitan Railway and initially ran trains between Paddington Station and Farringdon; two years later the main railway terminuses of Paddington, Euston, King's Cross and Liverpool Street had all been linked. Then in 1890 the first deep-level electric railway – what today is called the Tube – started running from King William Street in the City, beneath the river, to Stockwell in south London. Some of the earliest carriages from London's world-famous underground system, as well as examples of some of the thousands of Victorian horse-drawn omnibuses that swarmed the streets above, can be seen today at the **London Transport Museum** in Covent Garden.

Thanks to the Industrial Revolution, by the late nineteenth century Britain had not just the most advanced transport system, but also – for a few more years at least – the most sophisticated manufacturing industry, whose products the Great Exhibition of 1851 was intended to show off. London was the largest manufacturing city in the country, with a vast range of factories and trades, especially in the East End. The factories belched out massive quantities of filthy sulphurous smoke, depositing a layer of grime over all the buildings and noxious fumes in people's lungs. London's 'mysterious cloak' gave inspiration to painters such as the visiting Claude Monet; his canvases from around 1900, representing the Palace of Westminster and other Thames sites visible from his bedroom window at the Savoy Hotel, are rendered in garish colours that may seem unnaturally Gothic but were likely not that far from the daily discolorations of the city's atmosphere visible to the naked eye.

Further along the river there was frantic evidence of London's continuing status as Britain's trading hub, with imports coming in and exports going out through the many wharves around the

Pool of London. But by the early nineteenth century, the ships were getting larger and the river became ever more crowded with vessels whose cargoes needed protection from roaming gangs of thieves. So deeper, enclosed docks began to be built further downriver towards the sea, beginning in 1802 with the West India Dock, one of whose original warehouses is now the home of the Museum of London Docklands.

Other docks followed: the London Dock at Wapping in 1805 and the East India Dock in the same year; the Surrey Docks in 1807, the only one on the south side of the river; the Regent's Canal Dock (now Limehouse Basin) in 1820; and the furthest upriver, St Katharine Docks by Tower Bridge, in 1828. During Victoria's reign, three more were added further east, the Millwall Docks on the Isle of Dogs in 1868, and two gigantic docks on the edge of East London at Silvertown: the Royal Victoria Dock in 1855, today the home of the **ExCel Centre**, one of London's principal exhibition halls; and the Royal Albert Dock in 1880. In 1921, the King George V Dock was added beside it, and today the runway of **London City Airport** sits on the narrow strip of land dividing the two.

INTERLUDE: A LONDON LITERARY PUB CRAWL

London has some of the best pubs in Britain and a tour of these hostelries is one of the best ways to get acquainted with the life of the city and its people, provided you can stay sober in the process. The West End is particularly well provided with historic watering holes, where some of the city's greatest writers have propped up the bar on a regular basis. And the name that comes up again and again in numerous London pubs is Charles Dickens, who set parts of his novels in famous inns across the city, including the **George Inn** at Southwark, mentioned in *Little Dorrit*: a magnificent galleried coaching inn, one of the oldest in London, which is now owned by the National Trust.

Ye Olde Cheshire Cheese on Fleet Street was also used by Dickens as a setting, in this case in *A Tale of Two Cities*; besides, it was the regular rendezvous for a group of London-based poets in the 1890s, including the future Irish Nobel laureate W. B. Yeats, and was once frequented by Samuel Johnson, whose house, now a museum, is in Gough Square not far away. There has been a pub on the site of the Cheshire Cheese for many centuries, but the current one – a famously gloomy place with little natural light – was built in 1667, after its previous incarnation was destroyed by the Great Fire of the previous year.

Another pub nearby where Dickens used to drink is the **Lamb** in Lamb's Conduit Street, Bloomsbury, just a couple of streets away from the home he had in Doughty Street, which is now the **Charles Dickens Museum**. And somewhat further afield is the **Lamb and Flag**, in Rose Street in Covent Garden, which was another favourite haunt not only for Dickens but for writers across the centuries, including John Dryden in the late seventeenth century, who must have cottoned on to its pleasures shortly after it opened in 1688.

On the other side of Charing Cross Road, in Soho, just a short walk away (or by now perhaps a slightly tipsy stroll), we'll find the **Dog & Duck**, where Dante Gabriel Rossetti was once a patron, and where a century later George Orwell could often be seen unwinding while working at the BBC during World War Two. If he wasn't there, he could sometimes be found in the **Fitzroy Tavern** in Fitzrovia, just north of Soho on the other side of Oxford Street, where another regular was the poet Dylan Thomas, whose consumption of alcohol left everyone in his wake.

IMPERIAL LONDON: ... AND THE POVERTY

It was not just goods but also people that arrived at the London docks throughout the nineteenth century. Since the Glorious Revolution, the city's population had been increasing not just in size but also in variety. First, in the late seventeenth century, came Huguenots fleeing Catholic persecution in France; they established the silk-weaving trade in Spitalfields, east London, and made substantial contributions to the book trade, journalism, the arts and banking, but within a few generations they had ceased to exist as a separate religious and ethnic minority. Then throughout the next couple of centuries the spread of empire brought tens of thousands of immigrants from Africa and the Indian subcontinent to Britain, and especially to London. In the nineteenth century, poverty and economic opportunity brought large numbers of Irish immigrants and then a huge influx, as tens of thousands fled the Great Potato

Famine of the late 1840s, so that by 1851 the Irish population in the city exceeded 100,000 – nearly 5 per cent of the total. Germans also arrived – around 15,000 were living in London in 1861 – and then tens of thousands of Russian Jews fleeing the pogroms of the late nineteenth century, settling mostly in disease-ridden East End slums.

By the 1870s, the scale of human misery in the city's worst areas could no longer be ignored and, under pressure from social reformers, legislation was passed allowing notorious slums to be cleared and new estates to be built by private charitable foundations like the Peabody Trust. But with the population doubling in 40 years to more than six million by the end of Victoria's reign in 1901, it was not a quick fix. The following year the American writer Jack London, visiting the East End, saw conditions of extreme wretchedness. These had hardly changed since the French artist Gustave Doré had visited the city in the late 1860s and created haunting images such as the canvas *A Poor-House* (*c.*1869) – now in the collection of the Museum of London – or those in the book *London: A Pilgrimage* (1872), a collaboration with the English writer Blanchard Jerrold, which chronicled the desperation of the poor at length. As a result of such endemic misery, violent crime and prostitution were all too common, and in the late 1880s a series of violent murders of East End prostitutes sent shockwaves not only across the capital itself but around the world.

DISASTERS: JACK THE RIPPER

In 1888, Whitechapel was chronically overcrowded with mostly Jewish immigrants who often struggled to find employment. Many young women turned to prostitution to survive, which left them vulnerable to violent men at a time when women had few legal rights. That summer and autumn, a series of similar but increasingly brutal murders of prostitutes in a cluster of streets in the Whitechapel area led police to believe they were dealing with a single individual, though it was hard to be sure. Five such crimes, dating from 31 August to 9 November, exhibited increasing amounts of mutilation with everyone who has since examined the case in detail agreeing that they were committed by the same man. But there were other victims, too, both before and after the 'canonical five', as they are known, which might be attributed to him. The media frenzy in a new age of mass-circulation newspapers was exacerbated by the fact that, despite numerous suspects of all social classes, no one was ever charged for the crimes. To this day the identity of Jack the Ripper, as he was dubbed, is a mystery which has spawned any number of theories. Whoever he was, he could only have been responsible for a handful of the many violent murders that took place every year in the pestilential London slums. But worldwide horror at the savagery of these attacks did at least goad the authorities into renewed efforts to eradicate the terrible conditions in which the poor of London were forced to live.

ALONG THE RIVER: MILLENNIUM BRIDGE TO LONDON BRIDGE

Leaving behind the Millennium Bridge, we pass the new Globe Theatre at Bankside and then head under Southwark Bridge, built in 1913 to replace an earlier crossing of 1818. Almost immediately we reach the rail viaduct out of Cannon Street Station, and then on the south bank of the river – just after the notorious Clink Prison (today the **Clink Prison Museum**) from which a slang word for jail derives – we see the colourful, high, narrow stern of the **Golden Hinde II**: a replica of the galleon in which between 1577 and 1580 Sir Francis Drake and his crew circumnavigated the globe, which is sitting in dry dock as a tourist attraction.

Up ahead is the current bridge occupying the site where the Romans first spanned the river in the middle of the first century AD. For the next 1,700 years, until the building of Westminster Bridge in 1750, London Bridge was the only fixed crossing of the Thames in London, and today is known to children around the world through the nursery rhyme 'London Bridge is Falling Down'. In fact, after the Romans left, this was exactly what happened to it, along with the rest of London, and a new bridge was not built until the tenth century, after King Alfred had wrested back the city from the Danes. A few decades later, in 1014, it was deliberately burnt down in a defensive action by Olaf, King of Norway, who was helping the English King Æthelred the Unready in a desperate defence against Danish forces once again trying to occupy London; the ploy failed and Cnut, the Danish – and now English – king emerged victorious. Then, following the Conquest, William of Normandy again rebuilt it, only for a great storm to destroy it in 1091, a few years after the tyrant's death. The replacement – another wooden structure – was consumed by fire in 1136 and again rebuilt.

The medieval stone bridge that followed was commissioned by Henry II as an act of penance for the murder of the Archbishop of Canterbury, St Thomas Becket, and featured a chapel to the saint in the centre. This became the starting point for pilgrims setting out on the pilgrimage to Canterbury, which forms the backdrop to the greatest work of medieval literature in English: Geoffrey Chaucer's *Canterbury Tales*, first published in 1478 though written a century earlier. On either side of the Chapel of St Thomas, a dense forest of buildings, some as many as seven storeys high, grew up on the bridge, so that by the Tudor period there were some 200 buildings, mostly shops, along its narrow span. The wonderful modern scale model in the nearby Wren church of St Magnus the Martyr shows how Old London Bridge would have appeared around 1400. Among the many scenes it depicts, we see Henry V crossing with his entourage from the Southwark side, and the Lord Mayor coming out to meet him from the City; a freeman driving his sheep across the bridge, a right still reserved to freemen of the City of London today; numerous other livestock groups going one way or the other; and everywhere spectators, people fishing, shopping, repairing the bridge's foundations, unloading sacks of grain, and so on.

But with so much unregulated building and trading, the heavily congested bridge was a disaster waiting to happen. Already in the fire of 1212, just a few years after the bridge had been completed and before the building boom, fires had broken out at either end of the structure and killed hundreds if not thousands of people trapped in the middle. Then in 1666, a third of the houses at the northern end of the bridge were torched in the most infamous Great Fire, and in the following century for safety's sake those that remained were torn down by order of Parliament. In 1831, the old bridge was replaced by a new, much wider bridge, which stood for 140 years until the current, very functional structure replaced it.

PLAYING LONDON

Until 1672, when the composer John Banister organised the first public concerts ever given in England at his house in White Friars near Fleet Street, formal music-making had been largely either a private matter or an activity of court or church. Indeed, Henry VIII himself had been an enthusiastic musician and composer, and his patronage led to the flourishing musical culture of the Elizabethan city. A century later, after the ban on 'frivolous' public music-making during Cromwell's interregnum, musical life in London came fully into its own during the Restoration period and then the reign of William and Mary. It was then that the first great genius of English music, Henry Purcell, composed masterpieces in every recognised genre of the day, including secular odes and sacred choral anthems; incidental music for the theatre; the first English opera, *Dido and Aeneas* (1680), premiered in a girls' school in Chelsea in the late 1680s; and ceremonial music for royal occasions such as the funeral of Queen Mary in 1695.

In the following century, London's musical life was dominated by George Frideric Handel, brought to England from Hanover by George I when he inherited the throne of the United Kingdom in 1714. Handel was stupendously successful in his own lifetime as a composer of 29 sacred oratorios such as *Messiah* (1741), a perennial favourite with English choral societies, and 42 operas – pieces such as *Giulio Cesare* (1724) and *Xerxes* (1738) – which like most of his works were premiered in the capital. Two centuries later, Handel's anthem *Zadok the Priest* (1727) was heard by hundreds of millions of people around the world who watched the coronation of Queen Elizabeth II on television in June 1953, but the composer was also required to provide music for his own patron and king. Some of the most famous of these pieces today are the three *Water Music* suites, originally performed in 1717 by an orchestra on board a royal barge sailing along the Thames. The craft was heading upriver from Westminster to Vauxhall Gardens, the pleasure garden that first emerged in the Restoration period, which from around 1730 onwards became a mixed-media spectacle far ahead of its time, involving painting, architecture and musical performance, as well as innovative lighting, elaborate catering arrangements and fireworks: it was here that Handel's *Music for the Royal Fireworks*, a royal commission for George I's son, King George II, was first performed in 1749.

Handel is today remembered in two London museums. The first, the Foundling Museum in Bloomsbury, has the second-largest collection of Handeliana in the UK; Handel was a governor and benefactor of the Foundling Hospital, giving public concerts to help fund its work. The second is the wonderfully unexpected **Handel & Hendrix in London**, spread across two neighbouring townhouses in Brook Street in the West End: one occupied by Handel in the mid-eighteenth century and an upper-floor flat in the other where Jimmy Hendrix lived with his girlfriend in the late 1960s. Each part contains unique items of memorabilia, such as the first draft page of *Messiah* or the picture collection that Handel owned and, in the other flat, the acoustic guitar Hendrix played while he lived there, the red velvet jacket he wore in some of the most famous photos taken of him or, in his faithfully recreated bedroom, his favourite cuddly toy (which he called 'dog bear'). Hendrix took great inspiration from living next door to Handel's former home, and the surprising juxtaposition of two very different musical figures, two centuries apart, is typical of the cultural thrills in which eclectic modern London abounds.

After Handel, England was still able to attract composers of the stature of the Austrian Joseph Haydn, most of whose *London Symphonies* were composed in the 1790s while he was living in the city, where all were first performed. It was around this time that London's musical life moved from outdoor settings, such as Vauxhall Gardens or Ranelagh Gardens in Chelsea, to dedicated indoor concert halls. The venue of most of Haydn's premieres, the Hanover Square Rooms, was joined in the 1850s by the Crystal Palace, newly located in Sydenham. Then in 1893, the opening of the Queen's Hall in Langham Place, close to the site of BBC Broadcasting House, soon led to the inaugural season of what has since become arguably the greatest festival of classical music anywhere in the world.

ROYAL ALBERT HALL

From the moment it opened in 1871, it was obvious that the acoustics of the Royal Albert Hall simply didn't work. Located on Kensington High Street, opposite the Albert Memorial in Hyde Park, the new hall was designed by officers from the Royal Engineers, who took inspiration from the amphitheatres of the ancient world. But the building's great size and its very high ceiling, made even higher by a massive dome, created a disconcerting echo that spoiled most performances. Still, the impressive building did manage to attract some of the great musicians of the day, including the French organist–composer Camille Saint-Saëns, who gave a recital on the hall's gargantuan organ, known as the Voice of Jupiter, in the venue's opening season.

Despite various attempts to solve them, the acoustic problems remained, so that when the Queen's Hall at Langham Place opened in 1893, it quickly became the capital's principal classical music venue. This reputation was cemented with the inaugural season of promenade concerts just two years later – a ten-week series of cheap concerts that ran throughout the summer, as they have done ever since. No doubt they would still be held there today if the Luftwaffe had not destroyed the Queen's Hall during the terrible raid of 10 May 1941.

The following year the Proms, as they had become known, were held for the first time at the Albert Hall, and in 1949 the acoustic problems were alleviated by the suspension of a series of saucer-like discs from the dome above, creating a false ceiling that diffused the sound back to all parts of the cavernous auditorium. This novel solution also created a rather interesting visual installation, made all the more so in recent times by atmospheric use of coloured lights.

These days during most of the year, the hall is used in a variety of ways: aside from concerts of classical, pop and other kinds of music, there are also awards ceremonies, charity events, film screenings and circus spectaculars. But from mid-July to mid-September, the schedule is entirely given over to the festival for which the building is world-renowned. The BBC Proms, as they are now called – every concert is broadcast on BBC Radio 3 – is an international festival attracting the world's greatest orchestras and performers, including leading figures of world music, musical theatre or jazz. But it remains primarily a classical music festival featuring a mix of standard repertoire and a smaller number of contemporary pieces, some of them specially commissioned for the Proms.

The popular image of the Proms has always been the Last Night, which every year is broadcast on BBC television. Traditionally, it is an occasion for much festive waving of Union Jacks by the Promenaders – the diehard aficionados who occupy the standing area in front of the stage. But in September 2016, knowing the world would be watching just three months after the UK's vote to leave the European Union, the Promenaders took a stand. Many in the audience that evening were enthusiastically waving both the Union Flag and the circle of gold stars on a blue background that is the emblem of the EU – showing once again the streak of independence and internationalism that makes London such a special and welcoming place.

ROYAL OPERA HOUSE AT COVENT GARDEN

The Royal Opera House in Covent Garden is one of the world's greatest opera houses and the home of both the Royal Opera and the **Royal Ballet**. Originally the Theatre Royal, Covent Garden, the second of the patent theatres granted a licence by Charles II, in the eighteenth century it became an opera house where many of Handel's works were first performed. The first theatre burned down in 1808, and the second, designed by Sir Robert Smirke, opened the following year, though the hike in ticket prices needed to recoup the costs of rebuilding led to riots inside the theatre, known as the Old Price Riots, that went on every night for two months, until the former admission charges were restored.

The current name of Royal Opera House was adopted in 1892, since when it has staged major productions of standard operatic repertoire, including regular new productions of Wagner's *Ring* cycle, as well as performances of lesser-known operas and premieres of challenging contemporary works by the likes of Sir Harrison Birtwistle and Thomas Adès. The ROH has also attracted a long roll-call of the greatest international opera stars of every generation, from Maria Callas to Luciano Pavarotti to Angela Gheorghiu.

In the 1990s, the theatre was extensively remodelled and expanded, with the vaulting iron and glass Paul Hamlyn Hall – known as the Floral Hall and once part of the old Covent Garden flower market – now absorbed into the overall complex. An elegant glass-covered bridge spanning the short stretch across Floral Street connects the opera house with the adjacent Royal Ballet School. A company first formed in 1956, the Royal Ballet is world-famous for the legendary performances during the 1960s of Rudolf Nureyev and Margot Fonteyn but has had many outstanding dancers since then, including, most recently, Carlos Acosta and Sylvie Guillem.

LONDON COLISEUM

The London Coliseum on St Martin's Lane, between Covent Garden and Trafalgar Square, is the home of **English National Opera**, where all operas, whether by Mozart or Verdi, Debussy or Berg, are performed in English. The auditorium has the largest seating capacity, and the proscenium arch is the widest, of any London theatre. During the 1980s, ENO developed a reputation for challenging productions that were not to everyone's taste but were often memorable in theatrical terms. Indeed, productions such as the one by Jonathan Miller of

Verdi's *Rigoletto* (1851), reconceived as a tale of the Mafia in 1950s New York, cleared a path for the greater stylistic freedom that directors now enjoy. ENO has given us premieres of modern operas by British composers, as well as the first UK performances of works by the American composer Philip Glass, among other overseas names. It shares the Coliseum with the **English National Ballet.**

WIGMORE HALL

The Wigmore Hall in Wigmore Street, in the heart of the West End, is London's finest recital hall. Designed by Thomas Edward Collcutt, the architect responsible for the original Savoy Theatre, the Wigmore Hall opened in 1901 and was originally called the Bechstein Hall until the nationality of its owner, the German piano manufacturer C. Bechstein, and the passing of legislation in 1916 prohibiting 'trading with the enemy' forced the hall to close. Sold by public auction, it reopened the following year under the current name and since then it has continued to attract the best international musicians, from Sergey Prokofiev to Andrés Segovia; several of Benjamin Britten's chamber works were premiered at the venue. In fact, many of the greatest classical artists over the past century have formed close ties with a hall whose superb acoustics make it one of the leading venues for chamber music anywhere in the world.

ROYAL FESTIVAL HALL

In 1951, a century after the Great Exhibition, London hosted a second festival designed to promote British innovation in science, technology, architecture and the arts. The Festival of Britain, organised by the Labour government of Clement Attlee, was a cultural booster jab for a country still struggling to rebuild itself after World War Two, with rationing still three years away from being fully revoked. In fact, there were exhibitions all over the country and in different parts of London, but the centre of events was at the South Bank, close to Waterloo Station. Sadly, almost all the buildings and other facilities constructed for the festival were demolished on the orders of the Conservative government of Sir Winston Churchill, which took power later that year. The one that does survive, the Royal Festival Hall, is now regarded as a classic of post-war British modernism.

The Festival Hall was designed by Robert Matthew, chief architect with the London County Council at the time, and his assistant Leslie Martin. While the exterior is striking in its distinctiveness from the Neoclassical character of London's major buildings, such as Somerset House just across the Thames, the design of the spacious interior was a revelation when the building opened. The auditorium, with its cantilevered boxes on each side wall, was groundbreaking, though the acoustics were always very dry, with the lack of reverberation a particular problem for orchestral performances. To a certain extent, these issues were addressed by an extensive remodelling of the concert hall in the mid-2000s.

The Royal Festival Hall is now a component part of the Southbank Centre complex, which also includes the adjacent **Queen Elizabeth Hall** and **Purcell Room,** for large and small chamber ensembles respectively. They sit cheek by jowl with the **BFI Southbank**, a cinema complex showing the best of world cinema, and the **Hayward Gallery**, one of London's principal public galleries for contemporary art.

LONDON AND THE POST-WAR MUSIC BOOM

The explosion of youth culture that began in America in the mid-1950s quickly spread to Britain and particularly its capital. It wasn't long before the inventiveness of British and above all London bands was blazing a trail that the rest of the world would follow. Sixties giants The Rolling Stones, The Kinks and The Who, key names in rock or mod music – the latter a specifically London subculture – were succeeded in the 1970s by some of the most influential names in heavy, psychedelic or glam rock. Led Zeppelin, Pink Floyd, T. Rex, Queen, David Bowie, Elton John and Kate Bush all originated from London or its suburbs. In the late 1970s, punk was another major youth movement whose key bands – The Sex Pistols, The Clash, The Damned and neo-mods The Jam – also originated in the city. At the same time, heavy metal, a major genre which would long outlast punk's shooting star, was led by two London bands, Iron Maiden and Motörhead, while the 1980s saw a resurgence of industry- and airplay-friendly pop from the likes of Culture Club, George Michael and The Pet Shop Boys.

Britpop in the mid-1990s was in part a London phenomenon, with seminal band Blur exhibiting a London bolshiness that can be traced back through punk to The Rolling Stones and The Who. But the 1990s also saw the growth of numerous subgenres of electronic dance music – such as drum and bass, garage, dubstep and grime – which grew out of the rave scene that spontaneously appeared in abandoned industrial spaces in London, as well as rural sites in the Home Counties just beyond the capital's orbital motorway, the M25. From this scene, global figures like London-born artist Dizzee Rascal later emerged. Then in the mid- to late 2000s, two London women with huge voices became two of music's biggest global stars: Amy Winehouse, a great but tragic artist, and Adele, the stratospheric megastar of soul diva pop.

In terms of influence on 50-odd years of popular music history, it's quite a roll-call, and that's without factoring in those from elsewhere, such as Jimi Hendrix or The Beatles, who made their homes and their best music in the city. With the help of London producer George Martin, the Beatles recorded all but one of their albums at Abbey Road Studios in St John's Wood, north London. Every year, thousands of Beatles fans visiting the city make a pilgrimage to the famous zebra crossing outside the studio to have their photo taken while crossing it and to write their names on the wall in front of the building where so many classic albums have been recorded by so many bands. Needless to say, the studio repaints the wall on a regular basis.

100 CLUB

The 100 Club, located at 100 Oxford Street, has one of the longest histories of all London's popular music venues. It first opened in 1942 as the Feldman Swing Club and for three decades hosted some of the greatest names in US and British jazz, including Art Pepper, Benny Goodman, Johnny Dankworth and Louis Armstrong. Then in the 1970s, by now called the 100 Club, it became one of the leading punk venues in London and in 1976 hosted the first international punk festival. Punk bands continued to find a home there well into the 1980s, but jazz gigs are still a regular feature of the programme, along with blues, indie and rock.

RONNIE SCOTT'S

Ronnie Scott's Jazz Club opened in 1959 as the brainchild of two British saxophonists, Ronnie Scott and Pete King, in Gerrard Street in the heart of London's Chinatown before moving to Frith Street in Soho in 1967. The list of jazz legends who have played in either premises is long: from all-time greats such as Chet Baker, Ella Fitzgerald and Stan Getz to modern masters like

Wynton Marsalis, Chick Corea and Arturo Sandoval.

ROUNDHOUSE

The Roundhouse in Chalk Farm, north London, was originally, in 1847, a circular railway engine shed with a turntable to direct trains onto different tracks; but in 1964 it was turned into a unique performance space for both rock concerts and cutting-edge theatre. Until the 1980s, the Roundhouse played host to some of the great names in rock, including The Rolling Stones, Led Zeppelin, Pink Floyd, The Doors, David Bowie and The Clash. It was then closed for more than a decade but from 1996 the space has enjoyed a new variety of uses, with classical orchestra performances, awards ceremonies and the BBC Electric Proms being staged there, along with the annual month-long Apple iTunes Festival, which started in 2007.

EVENTIM APOLLO

With standing capacity of more than 5,000, the Eventim Apollo – first built in 1932 as a cinema, the Art Deco Gaumont Palace, and later known as the Hammersmith Odeon and then the Hammersmith Apollo – is the largest regular rock venue in London after the huge auditoria of Wembley Arena and the O2. Located inauspiciously beneath the Hammersmith Flyover in west London, over the past few decades this famous venue has hosted most of the greatest names in rock, from AC/DC to Depeche Mode.

WEMBLEY ARENA

Wembley Arena is the largest music venue in London after the O2. Built in 1934, it housed a swimming pool until the 1948 Olympic Games in London but was redesigned to accommodate various entertainment events, from sporting fixtures to music and comedy shows. With a seating capacity of 12,500, the venue continues to attract some of the biggest artists in pop and rock music. ABBA's Wembley shows in 1979 are legendary, having been captured on film and later released on DVD, while Prince played here no less than 35 times in the 1980s and 1990s, at the height of his fame.

EDWARDIAN LONDON

London in the first decade of the twentieth century was the biggest and most prosperous city on Earth, a stately imperial capital whose serene majesty is captured in *A London Symphony* (1913) by Ralph Vaughan Williams. Magnificent department stores such as Selfridges and Harrods, and luxurious new hotels such as the **Imperial**, the **Ritz** and the **Waldorf** (now the **Waldorf Hilton**) went up during the Edwardian era, though the last of these was only possible once the slums at Aldwych and Kingsway had been cleared. By then, London was a county divided into 28 separate boroughs (four more have been added since) plus the City of London; the authority conferred on the new London County Council enabled the longest and most extensive period of rebuilding since the decades after the Great Fire.

Alongside the improvement of housing stock, the early 1900s also saw a further revolution in transport, with the horse-drawn buses and hackney cabs of the late Victorian period gradually replaced by motorised equivalents, so that by the end of World

War One almost all horse-drawn vehicles had vanished from London's streets. The new petrol-engined cabs would eventually develop into the classic London taxi of the late 1950s, the Austin FX4, on which almost all designs since then have been based. But one transport innovation of the period intended to replace the older methods, the electric tram system that once served central London, has itself long since passed into history, having ceased to run as long ago as 1952. Part of the reason for its demise was the simultaneous growth in the much more rapid Underground network. In the years between 1890 and 1906, four new deep-tube lines – the Northern, Central, Bakerloo and Piccadilly – were added to the Metropolitan, Hammersmith and City, District and Circle lines, all 'cut and cover' lines built in the 1860s and 1870s. (Two further lines were opened long after World War Two: the Victoria line in 1968 and the Jubilee line in 1979.)

London was also a crucible of social reform in the Edwardian period. Democracy in the UK had been extremely corrupt and unrepresentative at the beginning of the nineteenth century; an Act of Parliament of 1884 granted the majority of the male population the right to vote, but still some 40 per cent of men were denied and, of course, all women. In the first decade of the twentieth century, a group of women began campaigning for female suffrage, using tactics that they knew would shock Edwardian society and place their cause firmly in the public eye. Led by mother and daughter Emmeline and Christabel Pankhurst, who lived in London, the Suffragettes, as they were dubbed, chained themselves to railings, bombed churches including Westminster Abbey and, when imprisoned, went on hunger strike to underline the seriousness of their cause. Then World War One saw women take up men's work in factories and public services, and in 1918 universal suffrage was finally granted, with parity between men and women being fully achieved in 1928.

During the same period, this large number of new voters was further added to by immigrants to the imperial metropolis, with London's population reaching some 7.5 million people by 1919, despite the imposition of the Aliens Act of 1905, which had severely restricted Jewish immigration into the city. By this time, London had lived through World War One – the Great War, as it was known at the time – the first conflict for nearly 900 years in which the capital itself had been directly threatened by a foreign power, as first Zeppelin airships then Gotha biplanes bombed the city. There were casualties from these raids, which shocked the nation, including 16 children killed when a school was hit. But the most terrible catastrophe to befall the capital during that conflict came about not because of enemy action but through a horrible accident for which war was to blame.

DISASTERS: THE SILVERTOWN EXPLOSION

Despite London being Britain's industrial hub, with around two-fifths of the city's workforce employed in manufacturing, the 1843 Metropolitan Building Act prohibited the production of noxious substances within the capital's existing boundaries. Thus Silvertown, next to the Royal Victoria Dock but outside the metropolitan area, became a favoured location for factories whose activities were explicitly geared to the war's most hazardous demands – producing caustic soda, sulphuric acid, petroleum, etc. – despite the surrounding neighbourhoods being full of dense rows of terraced houses.

The Western Front had turned into an attritional nightmare seemingly without end, requiring massively increased production of the most dangerous substances known in order simply to maintain position. In Silvertown, on 19 January 1917, a fire broke out in the early evening at the factory of Brunner, Mond & Co., which in 1915 had been co-opted into the production of TNT. Very soon, the fire detonated the 50 tons of TNT stored in railway goods wagons beside the factory, obliterating the plant and those members of the workforce who were there at that late hour. In all, 73 people were killed and more than 400 injured, and the surrounding district was devastated by the blast. It was not the biggest such explosion in Britain, even in World War One, but it was the largest ever to have happened in London, and the worst loss of life from a single event in hundreds of years until the horrors of the Blitz some two decades later.

ALONG THE RIVER: LONDON BRIDGE TO TOWER BRIDGE

On the Thames at low tide, close to London Bridge, it is common on a Sunday morning to see people with metal detectors or spades in their hands, scanning or digging at the mud on the foreshore. They call themselves Mudlarks, after the street urchins who did much the same thing in the nineteenth century, scavenging for things they could sell so that they and their families could eat. The members of today's Society of Thames Mudlarks, officially approved by the Museum of London and licensed for the task by the Port of London Authority, are searching for treasure of the historical kind; significant items in the museum's collection have been unearthed by these dedicated amateurs over the years.

The Mudlarks are just one example of London's old traditions enriching the life of the modern city in new ways, and the same could be said of the Company of Watermen and Lightermen: the ferrymen who since the Middle Ages have carried people across the river, especially in the centuries when London Bridge was the only permanent crossing on the tidal Thames. Later, during the boom in trade of the Georgian and Victorian eras, skilled lightermen – as these hauliers were known – were needed to transfer goods from ship to shore and vice versa. One such figure is seen plying his trade in a flat-bottomed barge, or lighter, in *Nocturne: Blue and*

Gold – Old Battersea Bridge (c.1872–75) by James Abbott McNeill Whistler. This and other night-time images by the American artist who made Victorian London his home are among the most atmospheric ever painted of the Thames. In more modern times, some former watermen or lightermen turned to running pleasure cruises along what is no longer the working river it once was.

And in 1999, the **Thames Clipper** waterbus service was introduced, which today operates a variety of routes including the long commuter service between Westminster and the former Royal Arsenal at Woolwich, on the eastern edge of south London. As it moves between London Bridge and the Tower of London, the clipper passes **HMS** *Belfast*, a Royal Navy cruiser that saw action throughout World War Two, moored in the Pool of London and accessible to visitors. Immediately past the ship is the Tower on the north bank, while on the Southwark side are the rather squat headquarters of the Mayor of London (different from the Lord Mayor), a political office created as recently as the year 2000. In 2016, the newly elected incumbent was Sadiq Khan, the first Muslim to hold the post.

However, the scene is dominated at this point by the neo-Gothic magnificence of one of London's most enduring icons: Tower Bridge. Opened in 1894, it was built to service the East End, but the Pool of London between the Tower and London Bridge was used by numerous tall-masted ships even in the age of steam – indeed it still is today – so the bridge had to be able to open to allow for this traffic. The design that was finally approved was the brainchild of Horace Jones, the City of London's in-house architect: a low-level bridge, its outer sections a suspension bridge with a central section that could be raised with steam power, using counterweights and following the bascule or see-saw principle. Built of steel clad with masonry and brickwork, at the time the impressive structure was the world's tallest opening bridge, though the lifting leaves took a mere 90 seconds to complete the action even then.

As in 1894 London's streets still thronged with horse-drawn vehicles, the bridge employed two men whose sole task was to sweep the lifting sections free of dung so that the leaves could be raised without raining horse poo down onto those waiting on the bridge's approach roads. In its opening year, it was raised some 6,000 times – about 18 times a day – and even today it is still lifted three times daily on average. The whole operation takes around five minutes and as such is a minor inconvenience for the busy London road traffic. And it comes with the compensation of seeing an engineering marvel being put through its paces while some tall-masted vessel from a bygone age sails between the bridge's iconic towers. One of the best viewpoints is from the high-level walkways built into the original design, which today have glass floor sections on which tourists can stand and watch the traffic or the river below flowing beneath their feet.

WALKING LONDON

London is unusually blessed with wide-open spaces in which body and mind exhausted or overstimulated by the city can find a bit of peace and quiet, and reacquaint themselves with each other. In fact, some 60 per cent of the city is classified as open space and around 47 per cent as green space. Making up a large part of this huge area are London's 3,000 parks – a staggering number. Many are small local spaces, which are nevertheless cherished by those who live by them, be they well-maintained landscape-garden parks, such as beautiful **Waterlow Park** in north London, or havens for wildlife such as **Camley Street Natural Park** right next to St Pancras International, a tiny 2-acre (less than a hectare) site in the heart of the city where rare warblers, buntings and even kingfishers have been seen. There are also great forest and woodland areas, such as **Sydenham Hill Wood** in southeast London and **Epping Forest**, a former royal forest, once vast but still covering a huge area of northeast London and Essex. And every part of London has a major urban park within walking distance, some of great size, such as **Crystal Palace Park** in southeast London, **Victoria Park** in Hackney, in the East End, **Alexandra Park** in north London or **Battersea Park** on the Thames in the south. **Holland Park** on Kensington High Street features a beautiful Japanese garden; at its southern edge is the new home for London's **Design Museum** in an imaginatively renovated 1960s building that used to house the old Commonwealth Institute.

But think of London parks and the names that immediately spring to mind are the famous Royal Parks – eight in all – most of them connected to one famously outdoorsy monarch: Henry VIII. Henry was born in Greenwich Palace, as were both his daughters, the future Queen Mary and Queen Elizabeth. The surrounding area became a royal reserve, into which he brought deer that he could hunt. Unlike some of the other designated Royal Parks, the deer remain in **Greenwich Park** today, so that you might even imagine yourself in the countryside until you take in the striking view of Canary Wharf just across the river. But even in the heart of London, green oases are built into the structure of the city, from beautiful garden squares like **Cavendish Square** next to Oxford Circus or restful **Lincoln's Inn Fields** to the string of ornamental gardens along the Victoria Embankment from the City to Westminster. And it is here, in Westminster, that the most famous of all London's parks can be found.

HYDE PARK AND KENSINGTON GARDENS

Hyde Park is another deer park created by Henry VIII to indulge his passion for hunting. The deer are long gone, and in their place there are wide-open spaces and some famous London sights, both old and new. One of these, **Speakers' Corner**, is in the park's northeastern corner, not far from **Marble Arch**, the triumphal arch designed by John Nash for Buckingham Palace but then moved to its current location in 1851. Occupying the old site of the Tyburn gallows, Speakers' Corner has been a place of mass public protests since the Chartists in the 1840s began the social movement that would lead eventually to universal suffrage after World War One. But the tradition of people standing on a 'soapbox', as they do today, and exercising their public right to speak on any subject that pleases them dates to a little later in the nineteenth century, since when famous figures to have fulminated in this location have included Karl Marx, Vladimir Ilyich Lenin and George Orwell. However, the most regular speakers, including some today who have been at it for years, are just ordinary – if sometimes quite eccentric – members of the public.

To the southwest is Hyde Park Corner, a busy roundabout with another triumphal arch, the **Wellington Arch**, on what is now a large traffic island that includes a number of other major war memorials. And in the park, beside the long lake known as the Serpentine, is the **Diana Memorial Fountain**, designed by American landscape artist Kathryn Gustafson in 2004. More of a stream than a fountain, it was intended as an accessible memorial to the People's Princess and, as such, members of the public are allowed to paddle in the water if they choose. In the adjoining Kensington Gardens is **Kensington Palace**, Diana's former home, where a collection of royal dresses that belonged to Diana, the Queen and the Queen's sister, Princess Margaret, can be seen in those areas accessible to the public.

Elsewhere in Kensington Gardens are the Albert Memorial, the statue of **Peter Pan** – a perennial favourite with the public – and the two **Serpentine Galleries**: among the best places to see contemporary art in London, partly because of the quality of the work and partly because of the wonderful park setting. Moreover, every summer since 2000, the Serpentine has selected a major international architect to design a temporary pavilion as a folly or summer house sited next to the main gallery and then dismantled at the end of the season. This annual commission has quickly become an important fixture in the architectural calendar and has spawned a series of fascinating spaces from modern masters such as Oscar Niemeyer, Frank Gehry and Zaha Hadid.

ST JAMES'S PARK

St James's Park was the first of the Royal Parks to be opened to the public and was originally created as yet another deer park by Henry VIII. A century later Charles II had the park extensively landscaped with avenues of trees and wide lawns, and in the 1830s it was remodelled again by John Nash for King William IV. But it was Charles who in the late seventeenth century received a gift from the Russian ambassador of a flock of pelicans – the ancestors of the birds that can still be seen in the park today. In fact, St James's is famous for its assortment of waterfowl species, including swans and geese of various kinds and all manner of ducks. Close to St James's Palace across the Mall and to Buckingham Palace at the end, the park is right in the heart of royal London. It also backs onto Horse Guards Parade, where the Trooping of the Colour ceremony takes place every year and where in 2012, the Olympic beach volleyball tournament was held.

GREEN PARK

Green Park, at only 16 hectares (39.5 acres) is the smallest of the Royal Parks; like St James's, its neighbour on the other side of the Mall, it was landscaped in the nineteenth century by John Nash. Once a haunt for highwaymen and thieves, then later a notorious duelling ground, it also became a popular site for firework displays during the eighteenth and nineteenth centuries. But it was still apparently a shady place even as late as the 1840s, when three separate, unsuccessful attempts were made to assassinate Queen Victoria while she rode in her carriage along Constitution Hill, the road that marks the park's border with the grounds and high wall of Buckingham Palace. At the western end of this road, the park narrows until it meets Hyde Park Corner, with all its war memorials, and there are more of them in this section of the park. They include the **RAF Bomber Command Memorial** unveiled in 2012: a sentimental work, given the subject matter, but a big hit with the public nonetheless.

REGENT'S PARK AND PRIMROSE HILL

After the Dissolution of the Monasteries, Henry VIII appropriated the area of land that today makes up Regent's Park to make yet another hunting park. At 197 hectares (487 acres) this is the largest of the central London parks and is named for the Prince Regent, the future King George IV, who in 1811 instructed John Nash to create a park complete with a palace and various villas. The palace and most of the villas were never built, but the grand terraces from Nash's plan around the southern part of the Outer Circle, the park's perimeter – many of them completed by Decimus Burton and others – are some of the grandest houses in London.

Curving around the park's northern edge is **Regent's Canal** which stretches from Paddington Basin in west London to **Limehouse Basin** in the east, where cargo brought by barges from all parts of England would once have been loaded onto ships. The canal enters the park by the Central London Mosque and slides quietly past the netted aviary at **London Zoo**, an institution whose famous former residents have included Guy the gorilla, Jumbo the elephant and Winnie the Canadian black bear, which inspired A. A. Milne to create Winnie the Pooh.

Just across the perimeter road to the north of London Zoo is Primrose Hill, which was also part of the land appropriated by Henry VIII. From the top of the hill, there is a fantastic, protected view over central London. And in the southern part of the park is a perfectly circular road known as the Inner Circle, within which can be found the exceedingly fragrant

Queen Mary's Garden – the largest rose garden in London – and the **Regent's Park Open Air Theatre**, the only professional outdoor theatre in Britain, whose programme runs from May to September and then goes on tour around the UK throughout the colder months.

RICHMOND PARK

Richmond Park, at 955 hectares (2,360 acres), is by far the largest of the Royal Parks and as such is the local park for people across a wide area of southwest London, from Kingston-Upon-Thames in the south to Mortlake in the north. It is famous for its herds of deer, though these were introduced not by Henry VIII but by Charles I, who in 1625 moved his court to Richmond Palace to escape the latest outbreak of plague to beset the city. It was Charles who, to stop the deer escaping, had the wall built which still encloses the park today, making it Britain's second-largest walled park. There are still an estimated 630 red and fallow deer resident there, along with a thriving colony of ring-necked parakeets.

There are also some 30 ponds in the park – some of them created by order of Charles II for the deer to drink from – as well as a number of enclosed woodlands, in particular the **Isabella Plantation**, which blooms in spectacular colours when the azaleas come into flower in the spring. The park is even big enough to accommodate an 18-hole golf course in its southeastern corner and is also home to several substantial buildings. One of these, **Pembroke Lodge**, was the home of nineteenth-century Prime Minister Lord John Russell and later his grandson, the philosopher Bertrand Russell; while, for the past 60 years **White Lodge**, a fine Palladian villa built as a hunting lodge for George II, has been the home of the Royal Ballet School.

BUSHY PARK

Bushy Park is less than half the size of Richmond Park but, at 450 hectares (1,112 acres), is still more than twice as big as any of the other Royal Parks. Also in southwest London – between Kingston and Hampton on the east and west, and Teddington and Hampton Court to the north and south – it is another of Henry VIII's deer parks. The main thoroughfare, Chestnut Avenue, is today's main road from Teddington to Hampton Court, designed in the late seventeenth century by Sir Christopher Wren. It includes a circular pond partway along, which today functions as a traffic roundabout. In the centre of the pond is the **Diana Fountain**, a golden statue originally made for Charles I by French sculptor Hubert Le Sueur, standing on a pedestal made of marble and stone which houses a fountain.

As with nearby Richmond Park, Bushy Park still contains herds of red and fallow deer roaming through extensive areas of long grass. And it, too, is still wild enough to give a sense of what Henry VIII must have seen when he charged through the park in pursuit of his quarry.

HAMPSTEAD HEATH

At 320 hectares (790 acres) Hampstead Heath in north London is one of the largest of the capital's parks, bounded by Hampstead to the west, Belsize Park to the south, and Highgate to the north and east. It rises to its highest point at Parliament Hill in the southern part of the heath, one of the highest points in London, offering magnificent views over the city. **Parliament Hill Lido**, in the heath's southern corner close to Gospel Oak train station, is an open-air swimming pool open all day long from May to September and on restricted hours during the rest of the year. But this is not the only area for swimming, as **Highgate Ponds** – also in this part of the park – comprise men's, women's and mixed bathing ponds. Neighbouring **Golders Hill Park** to the west also includes a small zoo.

The heath is a haven for both nature and culture. Unusual wildlife that can be found here includes native species, such as kingfishers and two types of bats, but also introduced animals such as terrapins and muntjac deer, as well as a colony of ring-necked parakeets. And in the northern corner of the heath is **Kenwood House**, a Neoclassical villa with a celebrated art collection including paintings by Rembrandt, Vermeer, Van Dyck, Turner and Frans Hals.

HIGHGATE CEMETERY

London has many beautiful old cemeteries but none as celebrated as Highgate Cemetery, just a short walk from the eastern edge of Hampstead Heath and right next to Waterlow Park. It is one of seven major cemeteries established in different parts of what were then London suburbs between 1832 and 1841 to cope with a rapidly increasing population. The **West Cemetery** in particular is renowned for its extraordinary funerary architecture, in particular the **Egyptian Avenue** and the **Circle of Lebanon** and **Terrace Catacombs**. But individual monuments, such as the mausoleum of newspaper proprietor Julius Beer and his daughter or the grave of nineteenth-century prizefighter Tom Sayers, are equally remarkable pieces of funerary sculpture, reminding us of an attitude to death and extravagant mourning which, led by Queen Victoria herself, was central to the British character during that period but seems anathema today.

Highgate is also well-known for the numbers of famous people buried there. Most renowned of all is Karl Marx, who lived in London from the age of 31 and wrote all of his major works in the city; Victorian London's extremes of wealth and poverty were what convinced him that capitalism was bound to fail in the end. He is buried in the **East Cemetery**, where cultural figures such as punk impresario Malcolm McLaren and *Hitchhiker's Guide* writer Douglas Adams can also be found. Famous figures buried in the West Cemetery include the poet Christina Rossetti, the scientist Michael Faraday and the painter Lucian Freud.

QUEEN ELIZABETH OLYMPIC PARK

The London 2012 Olympic Games were arguably London's finest hour in living memory and left a legacy of goodwill towards the city around the world for the welcome shown by Londoners and the sheer pizazz of the Games themselves – a feel-good factor that buoyed up the rest of Britain during a time of economic austerity that meant social hardship for many. But there was also the physical legacy of a brand-new park with world-class sporting facilities, including Zaha Hadid's superb **London Aquatics Centre**; the **Velodrome**, designed by Hopkins Architects and nicknamed 'the Pringle' on account of its upturned curving roof; the **Copper Box Arena**, now used for basketball, netball, badminton and a host of other sports; and the **Olympic Stadium** itself, designed by Populous and since August 2016 the home of West Ham United Football Club but still capable of being restored to for athletics use when required.

Between the stadium on one side and the massive new development of high-rise apartments and the Westfield Stratford City Shopping Centre on the other is the **ArcelorMittal Orbit**: a steel sculpture-cum-observation tower contorting upwards like a deformed spaghetti tree. Designed for the games by British artist Anish Kapoor, this gigantic modern folly was recently given an extra *raison d'être* with the addition of the world's tallest and longest slide – the signature work of German artist Carsten Höller – providing a more thrilling way to return to earth than simply trudging down the 455 stairs or taking the lift.

Running through the park is the River Lee, the watery thread that flows through the much larger linear park – the **Lee Valley Regional Park** – beginning up at Broxbourne in Hertfordshire, north of London, of which the Queen Elizabeth Olympic Park is the southernmost part. With so much construction ongoing and with the immature landscaping still bedding in, Olympic Park will probably take many years to feel like a restful environment as well as a leisure resource. But its sporting facilities are the best in Britain and some of the best in the world.

ROYAL BOTANIC GARDENS, KEW

Kew Gardens in southwest London is the most famous botanical garden in Britain, and houses the largest and most diverse collection of botanical and mycological specimens anywhere in the world. The Royal Botanic Gardens were founded in 1840 but in fact several of the buildings and famous trees were already well-established on the site by then. An exotic garden with a variety of structures had existed since the early Georgian period, with the **Chinese pagoda** and the **Orangery** that still stand in the grounds dating from 1762. By then, an even earlier building from 1631, known as the Dutch House, was an official royal residence, originally part of a much larger complex of buildings known as **Kew Palace** – the name given to the Dutch House today.

But the structures for which Kew Gardens is so famous are the great glasshouses built in the decades after the royals moved out. Outstanding amongst these are the **Palm House**, designed by Decimus Burton and iron founder Richard Turner, and the **Temperate House**, also by Burton and opened in 1862, which today is the largest surviving Victorian glasshouse in the world. In 1987, a third large glasshouse – the **Princess of Wales Conservatory** – housing plants from wet and dry tropical regions was opened by Princess Diana. And just to the west of the Temperate House is a building dedicated to the work of the remarkable Victorian botanical artist Marianne North, who for most of the last 20 years of her life travelled the world painting every botanical novelty she saw. The **Marianne North Gallery** was built in her own lifetime to house her pictures.

The outdoor gardens in which all these structures abide have gradually grown in size. After 1840, the existing gardens increased in area to 30 hectares (75 acres), while the arboretum grew to 109 hectares (270 acres) and then later to 121 hectares (300 acres); today, its oldest remaining trees – the famous maidenhair tree, the pagoda tree, the oriental plane, the black locust and the Caucasian elm – date back to 1762. In an effort to bring the public even closer to these botanical giants, in 2008 Kew opened a treetop walkway on which visitors can amble through the canopy and get a sense of the world that they may not have had since they were children.

LONDON WETLAND CENTRE

The London Wetland Centre, managed by the Wildfowl and Wetlands Trust, is a 42-hectare (105-acre) wetland reserve in Barnes, southwest London, occupying the site of the former Barn Elms Reservoirs, just downriver from Kew. Walking around the reserve – a mix of lakes, lagoons and marshland attracting a wide range of seasonal migrant birds, as well as resident species as shy as the bittern and the water rail – you would never know that the busy streets of Hammersmith and Fulham are just across the river. The London Wetland Centre is a haven not just for birds but for all kinds of beetles, butterflies, bees and other insects, as well as numerous varieties of wild flowers and fungi. A cherished oasis for Londoners, in 2012 it was voted Britain's favourite nature reserve.

CHELSEA PHYSIC GARDEN

Chelsea Physic Garden is a 1.4-hectare (3.5-acre) botanical garden in Chelsea, located between the Thames and the King's Road. Founded in 1673 as the Apothecaries' Garden, in the eighteenth century it became the most richly stocked botanical garden in the world and today holds some 5,000 different types of plant, with particular emphasis on medicinal plants or those with ethnobotanical interest. In the late seventeenth century the garden initiated a global seed exchange – the Index Seminum – which continues today, operating across 369 botanical gardens and universities in 37 countries. Thereafter, it played a key role in spreading significant plant species to different parts of the world, introducing rubber to Indonesia and cotton to what was then the colony of Georgia in the southern United States, and also bringing tea from China to India in portable glasshouses designed by Robert Fortune, one of the garden's celebrated former curators. Being so close to the river, Chelsea Physic Garden has a mild microclimate that makes it well suited to growing Mediterranean plants, including Britain's largest fruiting olive tree and the most northerly outdoor grapefruit tree.

LONDON BETWEEN THE WARS

London after World War One was a city of increasing modernity at the heart of an empire that was starting to decline. On the one hand, everything was new, from the increasing numbers of motorcars on the roads, to further clearance of inner-city slums and the building of new suburbs. This programme of housebuilding, which gathered pace in the 1930s, saw London's urban area double in size between 1919 and 1939, though the population itself grew by just a few hundred thousand – from about 7.5 million in 1921 to around eight million a decade later, where it more or less remained for decades to come. This new and better housing further away from the centre, coupled with improved public transport, led to the construction of new arterial roads, such as the North and South Circulars, around and into the city, as well as new industries in what had been peripheral and even rural areas not long before. The strikingly modern factories – some of them Art Deco classics, such as the **Hoover Building** or the **Gillette Building** – which grew up along the A40 or the Great West Road were filled by workers living in places that had been discrete little settlements since Saxon times but were now swallowed up by the urban sprawl. At the same time, the shift in population also led to a new breed of traveller to the city: the commuter. In 1933 Harry Beck produced the now famous Tube map, which rationalised the tangle of lines running beneath the capital's streets into an easily readable network of compelling geometry. A modernist design classic, it describes a city which was in fact a crucible of many other kinds of modernism, such as the literary visions in works as various as T. S. Eliot's long poem *The Waste Land* (1922), a mythic evocation of the modern city; Virginia Woolf's dreamlike wandering through the interwar metropolis in *Mrs Dalloway* (1925); and Aldous Huxley's suffocating science fiction of a future London in *Brave New World* (1932).

The British Empire had declined in power, with demands for self-determination increasing in some countries despite the apparent devotion to the imperial idea represented in the triumphant British Empire Exhibition at Wembley in 1924. At the same time America was rising, and in 1925 London was overtaken by New York City as the world's biggest and most prosperous city; the City of London had already lost the mantle of the world's leading financial centre. Still, the Port of London remained the largest dock complex in the world and the capital's biggest employer, with 100,000 people working there by 1930. And London remained at the forefront of technological change, with BBC Radio first broadcasting in 1922 on the site at Langham Place of what later became **Broadcasting House**. This classic Art Deco edifice, completed in 1932 but vastly expanded since the millennium, is now an integrated modern media centre following the consolidation of radio and television operations on this site.

BBC Television began broadcasting from **Alexandra Palace** in north London as early as 1936, but the television screen would not start to dominate people's lives until the 1950s. In the 1930s, the big screen was still in its heyday, as the cinema – along with other new leisure activities, such as dance halls and sports events – grew increasingly popular. Aided by radio broadcasts and cinema newsreels during this period, modern sporting institutions such as the FA Cup Final, the Wimbledon tennis championships and Test cricket at Lord's and the Oval – all based in London – became national obsessions. But these same news reports also showed Londoners a coming madness, which in the mid-1930s bedevilled the Jewish districts of the East End – in particular, on the day in October 1936 when 3,000 blackshirts led by Sir Oswald Mosley marched along Cable Street in Shadwell and were met by a 20,000-strong anti-Fascist alliance determined to stop them. The encounter flared into a riot, which has since become known as the Battle of Cable Street. Although that day the ordinary people of London had quashed the Fascist threat on the ground, within a few years the Nazi menace from the air would transfigure the city in a cauldron of fire.

DISASTERS:
THE BLITZ

Everyone in Britain knew that war was coming, and the London County Council began evacuating large numbers of children even before the British Government declared war on Germany on 3 September 1939. These evacuees were sent in their hundreds of thousands to rural locations around the country, but many were reluctant and, despite the warnings, a substantial number had returned to the capital by the following summer. Then on 7 September 1940, the long-feared bombing raids on London finally began.

Initially, they occurred in daylight, but following British victory in the Battle of Britain, the Luftwaffe switched in the main to night attacks, establishing a pattern that continued until the following spring. Although different parts of the capital were hit, these raids focused predominantly on the docks and the Port of London, the industrial areas of the East End, the railways and the City. Very soon, up to 150,000 people without adequate shelter – in fact just a fraction of the overall population of the city – began taking refuge in the Underground system each night. Among them was the sculptor Henry Moore, whose drawings of Londoners sleeping on the station platforms and even in the tunnels while the bombs rained down on the city above bear some of the most moving witness of the war.

Then, on 29 December 1940, came the most devastating raid of all. The City was attacked directly, creating a firestorm that tore through the capital's historic heart, now known as the Second Great Fire of London. It was on this night that news photographer Herbert Mason climbed up to the roof of the *Daily Mail* building in Fleet Street and took the iconic wartime image of the dome of St Paul's Cathedral surrounded by smoke and flames yet apparently untouched, as if protected by some magic spell. In the Square Mile around Wren's masterpiece, 19 churches had been destroyed, including 16 of Wren's own buildings. Elsewhere, most of the City's ancient guildhalls also perished. In all, close to a third of the City, mostly historic and religious structures, was destroyed. Thereafter, the bombing moved west to other parts of central London, as even Buckingham Palace was hit. The final raid, on 10 May 1941, was the worst of all, as more than 500 bombers hit targets all over the capital, including the House of Commons, whose burning roof collapsed. And then, with the Luftwaffe unable to keep up the onslaught and with German attention switching to war in Eastern Europe, for almost three years there were no more raids.

In fact, the survival of St Paul's in December 1940 was not quite the miracle it appeared: the British prime minister, Sir Winston Churchill, understood the cathedral's symbolic value as much as the Nazi strategists who were trying to destroy it, so he ordered all available resources to concentrate on saving it that night – even at the expense of many other historic structures, including the neighbouring Paternoster Row, which succumbed to the flames. Indeed, the unwavering morale of Londoners in their darkest hour was instilled in them, or at least stiffened, by Churchill, whose statue stands opposite the Houses of Parliament in Parliament Square. Just around the corner in King Charles Street, behind Her Majesty's Treasury, is the entrance to the **Churchill War Rooms**, previously the Cabinet War Rooms. From there the man most Brits regard as their greatest-ever leader led the conduct of the war and made the speeches, broadcast on the BBC, whose dogged delivery and unflinching resolve underpinned the determination of Britons, including Londoners, that they would prevail in the end. This same defiance and above all the fierce love Londoners had for their beleaguered city can be heard in eulogistic wartime songs such as Noël Coward's 'London Pride' (1941) and Hubert Gregg's 'Maybe It's Because I'm a Londoner' (1944).

And when the raids began again in early 1944 in a campaign now known as the Baby Blitz, followed by the terrifying strikes of some 2,500 V1 bombs and, from the autumn of that year, the futuristic threat of some 500

V2 rockets that got through, Londoners were mentally prepared to tough it out yet again. By the end of the war almost 30,000 Londoners had been killed, but once again London itself had survived.

ALONG THE RIVER: TOWER BRIDGE TO CANARY WHARF

Immediately after Tower Bridge we pass **St Katharine Docks**, designed by Thomas Telford and now a swanky marina, with warehouses converted into offices as well as retail and leisure space. A little further on we come to two of London's most historic pubs, the **Mayflower** at Rotherhithe to the south – from where in 1620 the Pilgrim Fathers set sail for the New World in their famous ship – and at Wapping to the north, the **Prospect of Whitby**, London's oldest riverside pub, dating back to 1520, with its sweeping views across the Thames. Then rounding the Rotherhithe peninsula, and the redeveloped Surrey Docks, we reach the gleaming towers of Canary Wharf on the Isle of Dogs: a huddle of skyscrapers which, by the mid-2000s, had established itself as one of modern London's most identifiable sights.

In 1981, following the closure of the West India Docks the previous year, the Conservative government of Margaret Thatcher created the London Docklands Development Corporation, which was charged with transforming the fortunes of what was then a post-industrial wasteland with high levels of unemployment and social deprivation. But the proximity of the City and the LDDC's own creation of the **Docklands Light**

Railway to directly connect the two districts made the Docklands area an attractive prospect, and in 1988 the site of today's Canary Wharf was sold to the Canadian property developer Olympia and York; three years later, the landmark tower **One Canada Square** was finished. By the middle of the 1990s, with demand for office space growing, a further stand of large, tall buildings was being planned, so that today, with 15 towers over 200 metres and eight over 400 metres – most of them built since the turn of the century – the area feels as close to a modern North American city as anywhere in Britain.

Canary Wharf has since become a symbol of the success of the finance industry in London, which – as it was a century ago – is once again the world's leading financial centre (though some doubt this pre-eminence can last in the wake of the Brexit vote). And the brazen example and runaway success of Canary Wharf was a kick up the backside for the City, which relaxed its own planning laws in response to this new competitor, resulting in the welter of glass towers that have sprung up in the Square Mile since the turn of the century. For many, the spirit of adventure embodied in these brash new buildings was what led to the financial crash of 2008 and made everyone poorer except the people who had caused it – namely, the banks and hedge funds headquartered in the City and at Canary Wharf. But, love it or loathe it, the financial sector has played a big hand in shaping not only the prosperity but also the urban character and even the values of London over the past three decades.

SHOPPING LONDON

Popular tradition has it that Napoleon once described the English as a nation of shopkeepers and that in doing so he was trying to insult them. Whether or not he actually made this remark, far from taking offence, the nation as a whole has tended to regard the supposed slur as a rather acute insight into its character.

So it is not surprising that London's principal attraction for many visitors, and also for many Brits, is the world-class shopping on offer across the city. And in this field as in so many others, London has often led the world. It was here, in Pall Mall in St James's, that in 1796 Harding, Howell & Co's Grand Fashionable Magazine, the world's first department store, opened its doors to the well-to-do women of Georgian London, where they could shop in comfort, unencumbered by the unwanted attentions of men.

Men would not be forever excluded from this world, though, as the technological innovations of the nineteenth century opened ever more markets, product lines and consumer groups to the wily entrepreneur. The Great Exhibition of 1851 showed affluent Victorians a bewildering range of things their money could buy and led to a further glut of department stores over the next few decades, such as Whiteley's in Queensway in 1863 and **John Lewis** in Oxford Street the following year. The former today is a shopping centre, an American invention, of which London now has a very large number. But the experience of these malls is much the same wherever you are in the world, whereas the great London stores are singular places, secular temples to what is perhaps the defining passion of our age.

HARRODS

Most London department stores had small beginnings, and this was certainly true for Harrods of Knightsbridge, which is still today both London's and Europe's largest store. Charles Henry Harrod established his first shop in Borough High Street in Southwark in 1824. After a couple of premises in the East End, in 1849 he moved his business to what was then the district of Brompton, today's Knightsbridge, anticipating with the foresight of a great entrepreneur the boom in trade that would accompany the opening of the Great Exhibition in nearby Hyde Park only two years later. He was right: by 1880, with Harrod's son Charles Digby Harrod now in charge, the general store had taken over several neighbouring premises and employed over 100 people.

A devastating fire three years later might have destroyed the business, but instead the firm enjoyed record sales that Christmas and in rapid time had moved into a new building erected on the same site. The store's reputation and fortunes continued to grow, and in 1894 the present building was begun. Designed by Charles William Stephens, this would come to feature cutting-edge developments in technology and design, such as the world's first escalator, installed in 1898, and then the magnificent Art Nouveau food halls, dating from the store's completion in 1905 and still a wonderful environment to shop in today.

Such opulent decoration was added to during the time of Mohamed Al-Fayed, the last owner before its current Qatari proprietors. At considerable cost, Al-Fayed had one ground-floor room redecorated in the style of an Ancient Egyptian mausoleum and then the entire escalator shaft covered from top floor to bottom with Egyptian-style relief carvings and statues, in deference to his own native background. The results are synthetic but spectacular, as if stepping onto a Hollywood film set. Like previous owners, Al-Fayed certainly had an instinct for the modern visitor experience, and for most this is not diminished by the presence at the bottom of the escalator of not one but two memorials to his son Dodi and the woman who died with him in a Paris road tunnel in August 1997: Diana, Princess of Wales. A collective shrine still maintained by the current owners, it also stands as a permanent rebuke to the British Royal Family, whom Al-Fayed still insists are responsible for the deaths.

In 2010, shortly before he sold the business, the still bitter owner announced that he had burnt the royal warrants the store had always enjoyed. Such an act, which in previous ages would have been deemed sacrilege, has done nothing to deter customers from coming. With 900,000 square metres of floor space and

330 separate departments, Harrods is twice as large as the UK's next-biggest department store, Selfridges of Oxford Street, and its old Latin motto, *Omnia Omnibus Ubique* – meaning 'All things for all people, everywhere' – is therefore no idle boast. Today more than ever the store is a honeypot for tourists from around the world with the money and the energy to spend on the luxury clothes, food and other goods to be found within this gargantuan Aladdin's cave.

SELFRIDGES

Selfridges on Oxford Street, London's ever-busy high street, is one of the largest and most famous department stores in the world. It was opened by American retail magnate Harry Gordon Selfridge in March 1909 and still boasts the original Beaux Arts shopfront and revolving doors. But the experience inside is utterly contemporary, with a vast floor space equivalent to six giant football pitches devoted to beauty, fashion, food and other modern luxury items.

It was Selfridge, a pioneer in the field of marketing, who came up with the phrase: 'The customer is always right.' Ever mindful of the customer experience, the modern store has at least one café or restaurant on almost every floor, while the food hall on the ground floor is home to more than half a dozen, including a champagne and oyster bar. In the 1920s, Selfridge opened a garden on the roof of the building, complete with a mini-golf course, an 'all-girl gun club' and spectacular views over London.

The store was bombed in World War Two and the roof garden badly damaged, and Selfridge vowed not to open it again. But in 2009, at a time of global financial turmoil, the modern store replanted the gardens and even installed a mini-boating lake with a lifeguard on hand should anyone get into trouble.

Once part of the same group as John Lewis, another of the great Oxford Street stores, Selfridges is now owned by Canadian businessman Galen Weston. In 2013, it received the best promotion possible when the British commercial television network, ITV, made a ten-part television series, *Mr Selfridge*, about its illustrious former owner and his store. There have since been three further series. Marketing doesn't get better than that.

LIBERTY

Liberty, with its tradition of internationalism, is perhaps the most quintessentially English of the great London department stores. It was opened in 1875 by English businessman Arthur Lasenby Liberty, at 218a Regent Street, a building that is no longer part of the Liberty site. Its current premises, opened in 1924, occupy an adjacent building on Great Marlborough Street which was designed by Edwin T. Hall in the Tudor Revival style that was fashionable in the 1920s. As if to enhance the sense that the shop is a world set apart from its urban surroundings, the timbers used to construct it came from two former warships of the Royal Navy, HMS *Impregnable* and HMS *Hindostan*. Most magical of all its seemingly antique spaces, the central atrium with glass roof at the heart of the store is one of London's most unexpected architectural wonders.

But while the illusion of a building from England's Elizabethan golden age is compelling for all but the most knowledgeable architectural critics, the shop still manages the unique balance between modernity and tradition which has always been its USP. Modernity can be found in the perfumes, cosmetics and eclectic range of high-end fashion by younger designers on their way up the career ladder. Tradition for Liberty means the vast and growing archive of Liberty prints, famous around the world, which customers can obtain in the form of scarves, bags, blouses, dresses, ties, shoes, wallpaper and, of course, the fabrics with which to make many of these items. These patterns are mostly provided by Liberty's own team of in-house designers, but the store has also been renowned since the early days for collaborating with international names from William Morris to Yves Saint Laurent. And the same internationalism can be also found in some of the store's longest-established departments, in particular the rug room, whose vast inventory of handmade rugs and carpets is sourced from expert artist-craftsmen across Asia and Africa, from Morocco to Turkmenistan and from India to Turkey.

FORTNUM & MASON

With its floor staff in red or black tailcoats, Fortnum & Mason on Piccadilly has the air of unchanging traditions, so it is no surprise to learn that the grocery store established on this site by William Fortnum and Hugh Mason first opened its doors in 1707. As such, Fortnum's is as much a British institution as it is a shop: world-renowned for its loose-leaf teas (among many other own-branded products), as well as its luxury picnic hampers, which for some people still constitute the ideal Christmas gift. And for many visitors to the capital, taking tea in Fortnum's fourth-floor Tea Salon is a time-honoured ritual not to be missed.

Curiously for such an upmarket store, Fortnum's was also the first retailer in Britain to sell Heinz baked beans; but then, one age's luxury item is another's grocery staple. And with plush pile carpet wherever you walk and classical music piped throughout the store, while surrounded by luxury foods of all kinds, the Fortnum's experience is certainly among the most old-fashioned pleasures to be had in contemporary London.

STREETS, ARCADES AND SQUARES

Of course, London shopping is not just about big stores, as some of the capital's most bespoke traditions are associated with particular streets or districts. Two of the most famous stem from the 1960s, the swinging decade in which London became the fashion and cultural capital of the world. The first, **Carnaby Street** just behind Regent Street in the West End, still actively celebrates its history as a centre of London fashion during that period, when it was home to leading British designers and a regular haunt of some of the hippest bands of the day, among them The Rolling Stones. In the 1980s this pedestrian street became associated with a new wave of British designers and then in the 2000s became a key location for British hip hop.

The other place is the **King's Road** in Chelsea, where Mary Quant, the inventor of the miniskirt, had her first shop and where mods in their fishtail parkas would ride up and down on their Vespa and Lambretta scooters, the chariots of their tribe. The King's Road also extended its own influence well into the 1970s, when Malcolm McLaren and his designer girlfriend Vivienne (now Dame Vivienne) Westwood opened the punk boutique SEX, which made the street a regular promenade for the movement's devotees, with their spiky-top or Mohican hairstyles, their bondage trousers and their tongue-in-cheek desire to shock.

Elsewhere, anyone wanting to buy haute couture directly from the couture house itself would head to **Sloane Street** – between Sloane Square to the south and Knightsbridge to the north – or to **Bond Street**, running between Oxford Street and Piccadilly. **Savile Row**, running parallel with Regent Street, is still home to a concentration of bespoke men's tailors, as it has been since the 1800s, while **Jermyn Street** in St James's is famous for the number of shirtmakers based there, some since the end of the nineteenth century.

In some places local trading patterns go back much further. **Hatton Garden**, running north from Holborn, has been London's jewellery quarter since the medieval period and today is still the centre of London's diamond trade. In other places, old traditions have given way to new uses, as in **Covent Garden**, which from

1654 to 1974 was home to central London's main fruit and vegetable and flower markets, until traffic congestion made conducting business close to impossible. The wholesalers' loss was the tourist's gain: the market moved to a site in Nine Elms, just south of the river, and in 1980 the central hall reopened as an atmospheric retail space featuring dozens of small businesses, both shops and restaurants, while the cobbled piazza surrounding it has become the busiest site for street performance anywhere in London.

The regeneration of Covent Garden also set the template for places like **Hay's Galleria** at Southwark or **Leadenhall Market** in the City across the river, a marvellous series of covered Victorian arcades designed in 1881 by Horace Jones and now home to a variety of retail outlets and places to eat. And there are wonderful covered arcades in the West End, too, in particular the **Burlington Arcade** off Piccadilly, between the Royal Academy and Bond Street, which has an atmosphere redolent of the elegant arcades of Paris.

LONDON'S MARKETS

London is known for liveliness rather than for elegance, and it's a quality that can be found above all in its many markets – several hundred across the city – from little street markets like **Berwick Street Market** in the West End to eclectic centres of world food like the **Southbank Market** outside the Royal Festival Hall and **Maltby Street Market** near London Bridge. Some of these centres of trade date back centuries, with **Smithfield Meat Market** near the Barbican, originally a live cattle market, going back more than a thousand years to the century before the Norman Conquest. **Borough Market**, near London Bridge, is almost as old and for much of its history was a wholesale fruit and vegetable market, though in recent years it has become renowned for its speciality foods, both ingredients and prepared meals. **Old Spitalfields Market** in the East End, again a covered former fruit and veg market, has occupied the same site for more than 350 years and today sells a mixture of things, including antiques, food and fashion by up-and-coming designers.

At **Camden Market** in north London all manner of things can be found – from food and music to clothes and bric-a-brac. In just a few decades it has grown to be perhaps the largest and most popular of all London's markets. In fact a series of markets, it is centred around **Camden Lock Market** on the Regent's Canal which passes through the area. **Portobello Road Market** began in the nineteenth century as a fruit and veg market and is still a street market today, but since the 1940s it has also been the best place in London to buy antiques, with an international reputation that draws people to the capital from all over the world. And **Columbia Road Market**, a Sunday market, has been running since Victorian times. Plants, flowers and bulbs are sold from the stalls, while the shops that line either side of the street offer artisan bread and cheese, antiques and garden accessories.

POST-WAR LONDON

London at the end of the war was a wounded city, with bomb sites and damaged buildings in every district but especially in the centre and to the east. These sites would be the subject of a huge reconstruction effort in the decades to come, as can be seen in paintings of such places from the 1950s by Frank Auerbach, a London Jewish painter who as a child before the war had fled the Nazis. Along with fellow Jewish refugee Londoner Lucian Freud, he became one of the leading British painters of the post-war generation.

The scale of the devastation – the worst since the Great Fire – at least gave the London County Council and various borough councils an incentive to clear away the last of the slums which had blighted the capital for nigh on two hundred years, replacing them with new estates of houses, which boasted affordable rents and all mod cons. New satellite towns were also built around the capital, and the Green Belt introduced to prevent further urban sprawl. However, life anywhere in an impoverished post-war Britain remained hard, with rationing of food and other staples such as clothing, soap and petrol. These emergency measures were gradually withdrawn as production increased, but staple foods such as meat were rationed until 1954. Having to endure such a grim regime over such a long period, which had also included the war years, was especially difficult for the younger generation, aware of how different life was on the other side of the Atlantic through the movies and the music that exerted such an influence on post-war British culture. Their frustrations were most trenchantly expressed by two London playwrights: first John Osborne in *Look Back in Anger* and then, with the unsettling ambiguity of true art, Harold Pinter, born and brought up in the East End, in plays like *The Birthday Party* (1958), *The Caretaker* (1960) and *The Homecoming* (1964).

The capital's workforce had been depleted by war losses and also by Londoners fleeing the devastated city for a more comfortable life in the new suburban towns. London was desperately in need of workers to keep the most basic infrastructure from falling apart. Thus, in the late 1940s immigrants from the West Indies, still part of an empire that was becoming politically and morally insupportable, began arriving in the UK to work for London Transport or as nurses for the newly created National Health Service. They were often employed as drivers or conductors on the electrified trolleybuses that remained in service until 1962 or, from 1956, on the new Routemaster diesel buses where Londoners could literally (and often rather dangerously) jump on board. (These post-war icons of the city were so beloved that after the last one left service in 2005, there was an immediate clamour to bring them back, resulting in the New Routemaster designed by Thomas Heatherwick, which entered service in February 2012, just in time for the Olympics later that year.)

In fact, there had been black Londoners in significant numbers since the eighteenth century – men such as the former slave-turned-businessman Olaudah Equiano, whose autobiography inspired the movement against slavery led by William Wilberforce and, ultimately, the legislation that ended British practice of the trade; or Ignatius Sancho, the composer, actor and writer who was the first black man to vote in a British election and whose portrait was painted by Thomas Gainsborough; or Mary Seacole, the nurse–entrepreneur who did much to help British soldiers in the Crimea and at the end of her life was a grand dame as admired and cherished as fellow Crimean veteran and fellow Londoner Florence Nightingale; or William Cuffay, the mixed-race Kentishman who was a leader of the Chartist movement of the 1840s, which in April 1848 marched in London for male suffrage among other reforms. By the early nineteenth century, Asians, too, were making their mark, with the first Indian restaurant in Britain, the Hindoostanee Coffee House in George Street near Portman Square being opened as long ago as 1810. Its owner was in fact a Bengali: a former captain of the East India Company called Sake Dean Mahomed, who among many other achievements also introduced the idea of shampooing to his adopted land.

But these many precedents notwithstanding, the arrival of SS *Empire Windrush* at Tilbury Docks in 1948 was a seminal moment in the story of London. The hope of the new arrivals and the pride they felt in belonging to an empire of which London was still the semi-mythical centre is most movingly demonstrated in a famous piece of Pathé news footage in which a clipped-toned reporter questions one of the new arrivals disembarking from the *Windrush* that day. The interviewee turns out to be the Trinidadian Calypso singer Lord Kitchener, who launches a cappella into 'London is the Place for Me' (1948), a song he has written for this special occasion and a panegyric to the city every bit as heartfelt as Noël Coward's wartime hymn.

The West Indian community moved into rundown houses in once well-to-do areas such as Notting Hill, Ladbroke Grove and Brixton, but were met with no small amount of hostility from resentful whites, culminating in the week-long Notting Hill riots of 1958 in which hundreds were injured and large numbers of properties damaged. But the immigrants kept arriving nonetheless, and various parts of London were transformed by these new cultures and groups, so that in subsequent decades places in the west like Southall, Hounslow and Wembley would be settled by large numbers of Asians from the Indian Subcontinent or fleeing Idi Amin's Uganda. Haringey would become home to a large Cypriot community escaping the conflict on Cyprus in the early 1970s, whereas Bangladeshis would settle around Whitechapel in the East End, and especially in Brick Lane, fleeing the natural and political upheavals that beset the new country of Bangladesh in the same period.

To begin with, these new arrivals came by boat but with the introduction of long-haul flights, from the 1970s onwards it was increasingly easy to fly to London from all parts of the world. By this time, the capital was served by several airports, which had all emerged in the post-war period: Heathrow in 1946, Gatwick, Luton and Stansted over the following decade or so, and finally London City Airport in the 1980s. But it was not only the social character of London that changed profoundly after the war. The wartime destruction of manufacturing industry by the Luftwaffe had caused many firms to move production out of London altogether, never to return. And though the Port of London recovered its position for a time, the loss of empire in the early 1960s drastically reduced the trade coming through the capital. By the late 1960s, with new container ports like Tilbury making the old docks redundant, the writing was on the wall, and by 1980, the last one – West India Docks – had closed and with it, Tilbury aside, London's principal trading strength for more than a thousand years had passed into history.

Given these challenges, it is perhaps surprising that in the mid-to late 1960s, London became the cultural capital of the world. The music scene of the 1950s, featuring low-key skiffle bands and then the rather tepid British form of rock 'n' roll, led to genuine innovations in the 1960s. At clubs like the 100 Club and the Marquee, strident bands like The Rolling Stones and The Who defined a new attitude not only to music, but also to life in general. 'Swinging London' – so described by *Time* magazine in April 1966 – embodied as much in the look of models such as Jean Shrimpton and Twiggy as in the music of the period, was in fact just the latest makeover of a city whose underlying character and spirit of place were much the same as they had always been. This was apparent above all in the music of The Kinks, a band from Muswell Hill in north London whose song 'Waterloo Sunset' (1967) is among the most sublime poems ever written to the city.

DISASTERS: THE GREAT SMOG

Even that hymn of praise begins with the words 'Dirty old river...' – and dirty it was, even in the 1960s, having been pronounced biologically dead in the previous decade. London was a very polluted city: the cleaned-up buildings of today were caked 50 years ago with centuries of grime deposited by the capital's foul and filthy air. This amounted to a health emergency which, like the Great Stink 100 years earlier, had been ignored for far too long. People simply accepted the thick, smoke-filled fogs as an intrinsic element of a London winter. In 1852, Dickens had described these fogs in the celebrated opening passages of *Bleak House* (1853), though he saw their murkiness as nothing beside the murky moral envelope of the London law courts explored in that book. Then Monet's images of the city from the turn of the twentieth century are saturated in a sulphurous Gothic fog that seems both romantic and suffocating at the same time. And even in 1937 the Americans George and Ira Gershwin were able to play on this stereotypical character in their song about a love-struck tourist in London, 'A Foggy Day (In London Town)'.

But there was nothing romantic about the dense smogs, the old mix of soot, seasonal fog and deadly sulphur dioxide – known as 'peasoupers', so thick were they – which descended on the capital with mortal effects in the winter months. Over the long weekend between Friday 5 and Tuesday 9 December 1952, a particularly dense smog that fell on the city killed some 4,000 people, and many thousands more perished from its lingering effects over the following few months. The Great Smog, as this acute event became known, led to the passing of the Clean Air Act of 1956 and then further legislation in 1968, though the last of the infamous London smogs came as late as 1974.

ALONG THE RIVER: CANARY WHARF TO *CUTTY SARK*

Leaving Canary Wharf behind, as we round the headland of the Isle of Dogs, we can see the now familiar sights of Greenwich on the southern bank, the most striking of which is London's famous museum ship: the *Cutty Sark*. This is the tea (and then wool) clipper built in 1869, whose speed across the seas is a symbol of the efficiency and romance of British Empire trade at its height. Sailing ships were eventually supplanted by steam vessels, but *Cutty Sark*, one of the fastest ships ever to travel by wind alone, stands as an elegant and much-visited monument to a bygone seafaring age.

In fact, the ship nearly perished a decade ago when, having closed for a multimillion-pound conservation programme, it succumbed to a mysterious fire that caused significant damage before being put out. Much of the decking, as well as other parts of the ship, had to be replaced, but remarkably – just four years later – the vessel reopened to the public in a spectacular if controversial new setting that allows visitors to walk beneath the hull.

GROWING LONDON

London's outward spread was stopped by the creation of the Green Belt in the later 1940s, so that Greater London is now contained within the orbital motorway that was built in the 1970s: the M25. But its growth upwards was another matter, and in the 1950s and 1960s vertical living was seen as the answer to housing shortages in various parts of the city. By the late 1960s, tower blocks had begun to acquire a bad reputation and many were carelessly constructed. The partial collapse in a gas explosion in 1968 of the 22-storey Ronan Point in Newham, east London, which killed five people, proved a watershed in the drive to build high. Nonetheless, significant high-rise buildings such as the 16-storey **Keeling House** in Bethnal Green in east London, designed by Sir Denys Lasdun and finished in 1957, and the Brutalist classic 31-storey **Trellick Tower** in Kensal Green in northwest London, designed by Ernő Goldfinger and completed in 1972, today are highly desirable places to live.

Trellick Tower was surpassed in height just a few years later by the three residential towers of the Barbican Estate, but already there were structures higher still, with the **BT Tower** in central London (the Post Office Tower as it was known) rising to a height of 171 metres in 1964. This was surpassed in 1980 by **Tower 42,** formerly known as the NatWest Tower – the first skyscraper in the City of London. And then came Canary Wharf and the glassy obelisk of One Canada Square, finished as long ago as 1991 but still the second-tallest building in the UK, followed since the millennium by the rash of new buildings whose biggest boast – Renzo Piano's **Shard** next to London Bridge – was finished in 2012.

The tallest building in the UK and in Western Europe, this surprisingly elegant sliver of a mega-building is visible from so many different parts of London that, like a real-life Tower of Isengard, it quickly imposed itself on the minds of Londoners, both as an impressive landmark and an irksome invasion of visual space. Indeed, one of the most surprising experiences to be had today when walking around the Square Mile is the sudden appearance of the signature towers of recent years – Kohn Pedersen Fox's 110 Bishopsgate (**the Heron Tower**), Norman Foster's 30 St Mary Axe (**the Gherkin**), Rogers Stirk Harbour & Partners' 122 Leadenhall Street (**the Cheesegrater**) and Rafael Viñoly's 20 Fenchurch Street (**the Walkie-Talkie**) – above eye level and between the Neoclassical blocks of the City of London's great institutions, which still accommodate the narrow, winding street plan of the medieval city. A constantly shifting contrast of old and new that is both fascinating and typical of the eclectic character of contemporary London, it is also a visual spectacle that is constantly being added to, with many more buildings of a similar scale due to be completed in the years ahead. Indeed, the number of new commercial and residential towers going up across London is truly bewildering, though the emphasis these days is on a level of luxury of which ordinary Londoners can only dream.

MODERN LONDON

In many ways, London's recent success is an astonishing turnaround, as by the early 1970s, despite the hip reputation it had gained during the previous decade, it was a city in trouble. The docks, hitherto the biggest employer, were closing with alarming rapidity and Londoners by the tens of thousands every year were leaving the city for new towns in the Home Counties surrounding the capital. The population of Greater London, which in 1951 had stood at more than eight million, by 1981 had declined to just over 6.5 million, with the most deserted areas being in the once well-to-do boroughs of Inner London. Such an atmosphere of deprivation can also be a spur to incredible creativity, but by the mid-1970s, the inventiveness of Pink Floyd and David Bowie was being supplanted by the authentic disillusion of punk, as London's youth stuck two fingers up at society. The song which has come to epitomise the movement's anti-establishment cynicism is The Sex Pistols' anti-monarchist anthem 'God Save the Queen', which in an act of the utmost insolence was released to coincide with the Queen's Diamond Jubilee celebrations in 1977 and was immediately banned from the airwaves by both the BBC and the Independent Broadcasting Authority – an instant guarantee of chart success. But songs such as The Jam's 'Down in the Tube Station at Midnight' (1978) and The Clash's 'London Calling' (1979) perhaps better capture the sense of desperation felt by the young in a city in which, during the infamous 'Winter of Discontent' of early 1979, uncollected rubbish lay piled high in the streets and the minority Labour government was defeated in a vote of no confidence that would lead to a general election victory for the new government of Margaret Thatcher later that year.

But if anyone had cause to feel disaffected in London during the 1970s and 1980s, it was the capital's immigrant communities, at the bottom of the pile for jobs and housing, and harassed by both right-wing groups like the National Front and the discriminatory practices of the Metropolitan Police. A generation later these would be branded institutionally racist by an inquiry into the force's handling of the investigation of the murder, in April 1993, of black southeast London teenager Stephen Lawrence. In 1981, these frustrations boiled over into riots on the streets of Brixton in south London, whose causes were made clear in the song 'Electric Avenue' (1982) by British Guianese immigrant Eddy Grant.

However, the government of the day had other priorities, as the emphasis was on individuals rather than communities or groups. And the figure that epitomised this change was the yuppie: the young urban professional who tended to work in the City of London, newly deregulated after the mid-1980s revolution known as Big Bang. Since then the focus on moneymaking has been both blessing and curse. It is London's fate, its eternal character, to be a trading city – a place where people come to make their fortunes – and the numbers don't lie: since 1981 the city's population has risen again so that it is now higher than at any time in the capital's long history. And the immigrant community, now such a big slice of the city's increasingly youthful demographic, has come to be the voice of London, with the global explosion of dance music over the past 30 years owing many of its genres to the inventiveness of Londoners, both black and white. Moreover, the lives of the citizens of modern London, one of the most multiracial and multicultural cities in the world, have also been reflected in some of the most significant British novels over the same period, from Hanif Kureishi's *The Buddha of Suburbia* (1990) to Zadie Smith's *White Teeth* (2000) to Monica Ali's *Brick Lane* (2003). This phenomenal change in the city's racial demographic, though not its intrinsic character, was summed up in what was perhaps the most glorious moment in its history since the VE Day celebrations at the end of World War Two. The opening ceremony of the 2012 Olympic Games was more than just a magical couple of hours that echoed across the following couple of weeks. In that one unforgettable event, London seemed united with Britain in a way that is only rarely the case, representing all that is best about the country – not only for the rest of the world but for the British themselves.

DISASTERS: TERRORISM

If the Olympics were a beacon of hope in the recent history of the city, the incident which above all others in recent memory has tested the resilience and optimism of Londoners was undoubtedly the bombings of 7 July 2005 in which, in four separate but coordinated attacks in central London – three on the Underground network and one on a bus in Tavistock Square – 52 people were killed and more than 700 injured. The realisation that life-loving London, in common with modern cities around the world, might be the object of murderous, suicidal hatred was a seismic shock, particularly to Londoners who were either too young or too newly arrived to remember the city's long history as a target for terrorism, going back at least as far as the failed Gunpowder Plot of 1605.

Whatever the cause, it has never justified the means, even when it was a desire for Home Rule for Ireland demanded by the nineteenth-century Fenians, whose 18-year campaign was the first ongoing terrorist threat in the city's history. Irish Republican attacks resumed again, many years after an independent Ireland had become a fact, in the months leading up to the outbreak of war in

1939. But they became more deadly than ever during the Troubles in Northern Ireland of the late twentieth century, a campaign of nearly 30 years and hundreds of separate attacks. This led to many deaths and many more injuries, in incidents including the now infamous killing of the Tory MP Airey Neave in March 1979; the slaughter of 11 members of the Household Cavalry and the Royal Green Jackets, along with seven horses, in the Hyde Park and Regent's Park bombings of July 1982; and the Harrods bombing of December 1983, in which six people were killed and 90 injured.

It is a terrible history but, to a greater or lesser extent, one held in common with cities everywhere. And as they did in 2005, so Londoners will respond to any future threat in the same spirit of togetherness and trust in the future that has seen them get through worse travails in the past.

ALONG THE RIVER: CUTTY SARK TO THE O2

No sooner have we left behind *Cutty Sark*'s elegant masts and Wren's Greenwich Hospital than another stand of masts appears ahead of us: the 12 yellow steel piers that hold up the roof of the O2 Arena, the world's largest indoor arena by floor space and, since 2008, the world's busiest music venue, too. It's an unlikely success story, as for several years after it had served its initial purpose, the Millennium Dome, as it was then known, looked like being one of the biggest white elephants in history.

In the mid-1990s, as the year 2000 approached, the Conservative government of John Major decided to mark the occasion with a new Festival of Britain-type event to be held in what was then a large area of industrial wasteland on the Greenwich Peninsula, which was still contaminated by toxic sludge from a gasworks which had closed just a decade earlier. Then in 1997, the incoming Labour government of Tony Blair decided to inflate the planned event into a grand spectacle whose glory would translate into electoral advantage for the party. The resulting exhibition, the Millennium Dome Experience, as it was first known, was dismissed by most critics but in fact those visitors who saw it mostly enjoyed it.

The building itself, designed by Richard Rogers, was better received. In particular, the domed roof – more or less the only part of the original structure that remains today – was seen as highly innovative as well as symbolically meaningful. Its western edge touches the meridian line measured from Greenwich Observatory to the south, with the 12 piers that support the roof representing the 12 hours of the day or those on the face of a clock.

After the closure of the year-long exhibition, the building lay mostly empty for several years until a buyer was found and the Dome was given a new purpose as London's biggest concert arena. Today, in addition to being the world's most well-attended music venue, the O2 has a cinema, exhibition space, a music club and various bars and restaurants within the remodelled interior. It also hosts the annual end-of-year ATP Finals, a major tennis tournament, and in 2012 was the venue for artistic gymnastics and basketball at the London Olympics, as well as wheelchair basketball in the subsequent Paralympic Games. The O2 can be reached by tube to North Greenwich station or by yet another form of London transportation: the Emirates Air Line cable car, which glides over the Thames between the Royal Victoria Dock and the O2.

POMP AND CIRCUMSTANCE: THE SURVIVAL OF THE HOUSE OF WINDSOR

Like the Thames, the city's great buildings and the people who live and work among them, the Royal Family is a thread of continuity which, perhaps more for visitors than for locals, makes London what it is. The Windsors are one of the first things people around the world associate with the city, though many Londoners themselves are more ambivalent about the institution of monarchy.

This innate suspicion goes back centuries to those times in history when the people 'took back control' from monarchs who overreached themselves, such as King John, who in 1215 was obliged to concede the position of an elected mayor to the City of London in the weeks before the most historic concessions of all, enshrined in Magna Carta. The long-standing tradition that sees the monarch halting at Temple Bar in Fleet Street to ask permission of the Lord Mayor to enter the City may date from this time. In a similar way, in a ceremony stemming from Charles I's unconstitutional attempt in 1642 to arrest five Members of Parliament after entering the House of Commons without permission, every year at the state opening of Parliament, an official of the House of Lords – the Gentleman Usher of the Black Rod, otherwise known as Black Rod – approaches the House of Commons ahead of the Sovereign only to have the doors of the chamber slammed in his face. With his ebony staff, the black rod, he then strikes the door three times, requesting the House's permission for the Queen to enter and address them.

Ancient ceremonies such as these point to the longevity of British institutions but also the great age of Britain's democracy, with the monarch having long since been relegated to a ceremonial role. Indeed, without that function as the people's foil, it is not idle to speculate whether the monarchy would not have survived into the current century. Looked at from their nadir of two decades ago, it is a surprise to see that – after various failed marriages, numerous public controversies and above all the death of Diana, Princess of Wales – the royals have not only weathered all those troubles but embraced life in the twenty-first century in a way that few would have predicted back then. Indeed, the younger royals are as popular and as typical of their generation of Londoners as it is possible for people in their privileged position to be – just as the Queen was when she and her sister, by staying in London throughout the Blitz, gave such a crucial boost to the morale of Londoners during World War Two.

ALONG THE RIVER: THE O2 TO THE THAMES BARRIER

But the longevity of the River Thames dwarfs even the unbroken line of kings and queens who for a thousand years have reigned over the nation from the palaces of London. And as we leave the O2 and pass the royal docks on the north bank, ahead of us is the Thames Barrier. Its hollow stainless-steel piers, stretching like a string of silver charms from Silvertown on the north bank to Woolwich on the south, were built in 1984 to protect the capital against the kind of storm surge that hit the whole east coast of Britain in the winter of 1953.

On that occasion, over a single night on 31 January, the North Sea flood, as it became known, killed more than 300 people from Scotland down to Essex, flooding large areas including significant parts of east London. With the closure of the docks by the early 1980s, and the removal of large shipping to Tilbury further east, a flood defence system became feasible and was seen as increasingly necessary. It has been used more than 170 times in the 32 years since it opened – twice the usage envisaged when it was built – and especially at those times when a high inward tide coincides with heavy rainfall, thus bringing more water than usual downriver to the sea. How long the barrier will continue to protect the capital against the measurable threat of sea levels set to keep rising in the coming decades is a question that has been keenly debated in recent years. It seems likely that before the end of the current century an even more imposing obstacle will need to be constructed to keep London's many low-lying areas from disappearing beneath the water.

Indeed, anyone planning a new city today would probably think twice about siting it on the banks of a tidal river. But that river is not just a physical presence; it is the ebbing and flowing heart of London, coursing through the literature of the city from Sir Edmund Spenser's 'Sweet Thames' in the first Elizabethan age to Ewan MacColl's in the second. In between, as the metropolis grew, it had turned into an infested sewer in which nothing could survive, so that by the 1950s it had become a symbol for the city's decline. And that perhaps is the most positive indicator of London's revival of the past few decades. Clean again, the river today is home to all manner of life including 125 species of fish, as well as birds such as herons and cormorants, and mammals such as seals and porpoises, which feed on them.

One of London's chief pleasures is simply to walk along the riverbank at the numerous places where pedestrian access has been so much improved over the past 30 years – or across the city's many bridges. Perhaps for a minute we could stand on one and look back upriver, remembering Rudyard Kipling's poem 'The River's Tale' (1911), in which London's inscrutable historian gives up its ancient secrets, as if only the eternal Thames could grasp the true significance of the great and splendid city which has grown up along its banks.

ACKNOWLEDGEMENTS

It is quite a privilege to be asked to tell the story of a great city like London and to get to choose your own cultural highlights in doing it. So I owe a great debt of thanks to Claire Plimmer for commissioning me to write the book in the first place and for her positive reaction to the typescript I delivered; to Abi McMahon for tactfully and skilfully steering the project along its appointed course; to Jennifer Barclay for editing the book with such a finely judged balance of rigour and enthusiasm; and to Daniela Nava for copy-editing the text with exemplary care.

A CELEBRATION OF THE
KINGS AND QUEENS OF BRITAIN

FOR THE LOVE OF THE

ROYAL FAMILY

A COMPANION

Dieu et mon droit

ROGER BRYAN

FOR THE LOVE OF THE ROYAL FAMILY

Roger Bryan

ISBN: 978-1-84953-926-5

Hardback

£9.99

Did you know...

- William IV was wont to speak his mind and could sometimes lack tact, which is said to have inspired the nickname 'Silly Billy'?
- Edward III banned all sports, including football, on Sundays, so that his subjects could be free to concentrate solely on their archery?
- Coronation chicken was invented for foreign guests to enjoy at Elizabeth II's coronation?

This rich miscellany celebrates the fascinating history of the British Royal Family, from the reign of Egbert, King of Wessex, to the monarchy of the present day. Full of titillating trivia, little-known facts, bite-size biographies and memorable quotations, it paints a colourful picture of how the kings and queens of this noble land have shaped the way we live today.

Have you enjoyed this book?
If so, why not write a review on your favourite website?

If you're interested in finding out more about our books,
find us on Facebook at **Summersdale Publishers** and
follow us on Twitter at **@Summersdale**.

Thanks very much for buying this Summersdale book.

www.summersdale.com